What people are saying about
YOU WILL BE OKAY

Young people

'I have had quite a hard time with it [grief] and haven't really opened up but reading You Will Be Okay has made me see different views and ways to go about it. A book that definitely gets the emotions working and makes me think back to the times I had with my mum. I really appreciated the fact that the book talked about the future – I think it will really help me.'
Sam

'It would have been an enormous help to have had a book like this when dad died. It's a FANTASTIC book! I absolutely loved it. I laughed, I cried, and found bits of it really hitting home. Such an important book for all ages.'
Zoe

'You Will Be Okay really captures so many of the feelings experienced during grief and explains them in such a simple way. I think it is so important to have someone confirm that what you are feeling isn't "wrong" or "strange" or "weak" and this book does an excellent job of that.'
Emily

Parents

'I loved the stories; it was as if Julie was reading to me as well as my three children. The author's unparalleled experience of guiding families through grief is so clearly and honestly written. Without a hint of condescension, this is an invaluable blend of analogies, stories and exercises to help children navigate and manage their grief.'
Anthony, father

'As a mum of three children who all reacted in such different ways, I simply loved the idea of the 'grief muscles' to strengthen them after their dad's death. The book feels like a natural discussion.'
Kath, mother

'I loved this book and am sure that it will be a terrific self-help book for this age group for many years to come. I particularly love the case studies – such a diverse group of people who all have very different bereavement stories, but all have the same volcano to conquer, just like real life.'
Sue, mother

'We loved this book and wish I could have read it a few years ago when our son died. It has given us renewed confidence and understanding to talk openly with our children about their grief.'
Bill and Claire, parents

ABCs (Adults Bereaved in Childhood)

'My mother died when I was six and really this book contains everything that I now realise I needed. You Will Be Okay is a positive and honest directory of help for children and their closest adults when the worst happens. I wish my father had read this book when my mother died.'
David

'Wonderful writing with deep authenticity and a connection to children navigating loss that just can't be feigned. Children were sometimes made to feel that they should not talk about the person who has died as it could upset the people who they love and depend on. Better to be quiet and not kick off. I am reading this many decades after my mum died and I still loved it and found it helpful.'
John

'This book is a piece of heartfelt magic. I absorbed every word. If only Julie's care, experience and wisdom were there for all to read back in the 1970s – I think my life could have been very different!'
Sarah

Professionals

'I think [this book] will transform lives and should be on every bookshelf in every classroom. I am absolutely overwhelmed with the frank, honest discussions as well as the way it makes difficult topics and concepts easy to understand for the average 8–12-year-old (although I would say this book can comfortably be read by teens). The 'go-to' book for anyone dealing with bereavement at a young age.'
Alison Hopton – Deputy Head Teacher

'I LOVE it! Young people will absolutely know that Julie is an authentic partner who can be fully trusted.'
David Trickey – Clinical Psychologist and Trauma Specialist

'For the over one in 10 children experiencing bereavement every year; for the many children saying they want to help their bereaved friend but don't know how; and for those adults who stay silent because they can't find the words ... Julie Stokes has come to the rescue. Julie's book takes the hands of all those affected by grief and helps steer them on their journey to make their grief more bearable.'
Jackie Brock – Chief Executive, Children in Scotland

'As a play therapist supporting children and young people navigating grief in many forms, I am grateful for this resource that I can recommend to families and can apply directly in my work. You Will Be Okay beautifully captures the complexity of grief while providing creative tools and coping skills.'
Grace Deegan – Play therapist

'This is a wonderful book – Julie's style is so gentle yet focussed and the book is very well structured, wise and positive – another great contribution to bereavement care.'
Dr Marilyn Relf – Chair of the National Bereavement Alliance

'This book is like coming home. It will be an invaluable resource for families, young people and practitioners.'
Anita Hicks and Karen Codd – Clinical Leads and Co-Founders of Sandy Bear children's bereavement charity, Wales

YOU WILL BE OKAY

JULIE STOKES

ILLUSTRATED BY LAURÈNE BOGLIO

wren
&rook

First published in Great Britain in 2021 by Wren & Rook

ISBN: 978 1 5263 6389 3
E-book ISBN: 978 1 5263 6388 6

10 9 8 7

Wren & Rook
An imprint of
Hachette Children's Group
Part of Hodder & Stoughton
Carmelite House
50 Victoria Embankment
London EC4Y 0DZ

An Hachette UK Company
www.hachette.co.uk
www.hachettechildrens.co.uk

Editorial Director: Laura Horsley
Senior Editor: Sadie Smith
Art Director: Laura Hambleton
Designed by Kathryn Slack

Printed in the United Kingdom

YOU WILL be OKAY

Find strength, stay hopeful and get to grips with grief

For Frederick George Stokes,
my Grandad.

My first experience of being so shocked
and overwhelmed by grief.

We walked, talked and shared stories.

I trusted him completely.
Then, now and always.

J.S.

CONTENTS

When SOMEONE you know has died, it's a real SHOCK isn't it?

INTRODUCTION

I wonder how you feel right now as you start to read this book, at this time in your life. A book you never imagined reading about a person who was very important in your life. And what is your life like these days? Do you sometimes feel a bit sad, angry, confused, maybe even a little lonely or guilty? Perhaps you are showing those feelings lots. Or maybe you are trying to keep them under wraps...

Someone who WAS alive in your life has died, and they are NOT coming back.

What a  thing to say.

It is no wonder that something so big comes with very big emotions and so often we are lost for words on how to describe it all. Getting to grips with grief can be tricky, like keeping a boat going forward in stormy waters. Something that feels so unfair has happened and your life is turned upside down and inside out.

Imagine yourself in that little boat on the front cover trying to find your way through a storm. Only you will find your way through. This book will give you some ideas to help you to guide yourself towards calmer waters. It's a space for you to cherish special memories of the person who has died and give yourself time to remember them alongside rebuilding your life without them. It's full of interesting tools and tips for finding your inner strength, staying hopeful and looking towards the future. It is also a super-safe space for you to be able to explore, express and communicate exactly what you are thinking and how you are feeling. **No need to hold back here**.

The future can seem a way off, so trust me when I say:

✳ You will not always feel like grief is a hard lump in your throat that leaves you lost for words or feeling different.

✳ You will not always feel sad or angry when good things happen (because your person is not here to see and share it with you).

✳ You will get skilled and stronger at growing up with grief and this mindset will help you with other aspects of your life.

✳ You will accept that you did nothing to cause their death and slowly you will begin to feel happier with life.

✳ You will find that having fun comes back and stays for longer. It does not mean you love the person who has died any less.

So, are you ready? <u>Let's go</u>.

Getting to grips with grief

Let's start with the important bit. Who has died?

Is it your mum, your dad, your brother or sister? Perhaps it was a friend or your grandad or grandma, or someone else who was really important to you, such as a teacher or a family friend?

Maybe you loved them lots, or just sometimes, or maybe you didn't love them at all. Maybe you did love them deep down, but you didn't always like the way they behaved towards you or others. Whatever your relationship, they were still important, and they always will be an important part of your life story and who you are. So, it is natural to miss them.

They have died and you're experiencing something called **grief**. What do we mean when we say grief? Well, grief comes from the Latin word *gravare* which means a **heavy** burden. So, grief often results in heavy feelings, especially ones of great sadness. These emotions can also feel physically painful – sometimes it can feel like a large weight on your chest and other areas of your body. Just like the waves in the sea, feelings come and go. Some days the waves of emotions are gentle and other days they are gigantic and overwhelming.

Getting to grips with all your thoughts and feelings isn't over in a few months.

It's more like a long never-ending path, **especially** in the **early** days.

It gets easier to walk on, yet in the beginning there are lots of ...

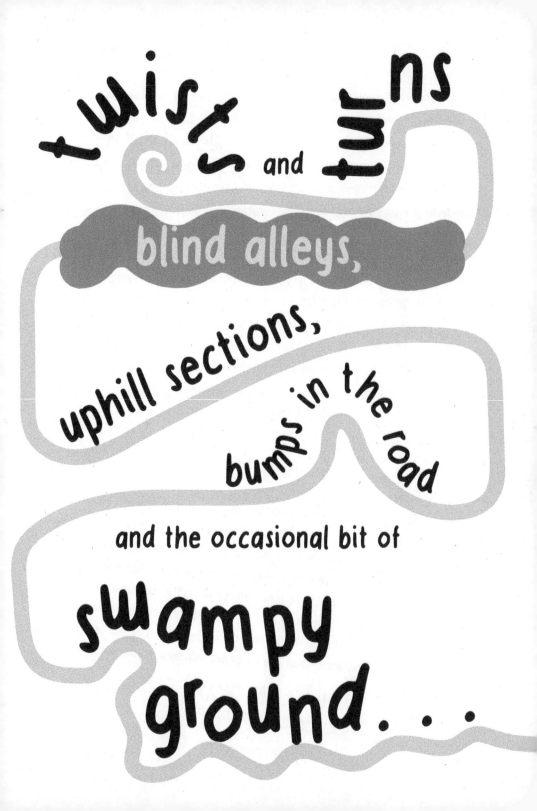

twists and turns

blind alleys,

uphill sections,

bumps in the road

and the occasional bit of

swampy
ground. . . .

So, some days you might feel okay and on others it can seem like everything is just too much and it's hard to find the strength to battle through – you are facing a raging **storm of grief**. But just as in nature, even bad storms always blow over. Some of the exercises in this book are a bit like giving you an oar or a lifebelt to help you on your way to calmer waters.

I will be honest with you, getting to grips with all these thoughts and heavy feelings is going to take quite some time. The weight of grief can be especially intense in the early days, weeks and months after someone has died. It's also a bit unpredictable, and although it does gradually become calmer and more familiar, it never goes away completely. In the beginning there is often a lot of confusion, anger, sadness and tears. Someone once said to me that with grief, although you never really **get over it**, you can become much more **used** to it.

You might be wondering who I am and why I seem to know about grief. Well, for a long time I've been supporting lots of children and young people, just like you, who have had a close family member or friend die. I have also worked with their parents. Along the way we've found things that have really helped navigate grief, and we have found things that don't work so well. I have listened carefully to very different experiences, and I will share some stories because grief can feel like a very lonely experience. What has happened will change you, but ...

YOU WILL BE OKAY.

My hope is that you will feel understood, more supported and able to recognise the thoughts and feelings of grief. You can slowly accept that the death is real and begin to talk about it more confidently with others. And most of all, that you are still able to have fun, enjoy your life and begin to feel excited about your future again.

There are no simple solutions because everyone's family set up is so unique, **you are so unique**, but together we will look at the clever ways you can hold on to good memories and keep them close. We will also discover ways of managing the memories that are more painful.

I will introduce you to seven important **grief 'muscles'** that you can start building and flexing, so that when you are feeling overwhelmed and lost, you will have the strength to see a way through to more solid ground. We will think about how your life might have changed, how you can cope with these changes and how you can adapt to any uncertainty you may be feeling. Plus, we'll look at how you can handle those awkward and embarrassing questions you might get asked along the way. We'll also meet lots of young people and grown-ups who have experienced the death of someone important to them when they were young. Some of the people we meet are quite well-known and it's interesting to discover some of the incredible things they have done with their lives. I hope these stories will inspire you, support you and remind you of your strength as you are growing up with grief.

Courageous conversations

So you are now part of a group of people who know what it is like to encounter death while growing up. It may have been a sudden death or maybe someone was ill for quite a while. It may have been suicide or perhaps a murder. Whether you expected the death because you knew they were ill or it has come suddenly – pretty much everyone says it feels like a **complete shock** that they never expected to happen so early on in their life.

You might be surprised at how often family members, your teachers or other adults in your life might change the subject to avoid talking about what has happened. It can all be quite confusing. That's because most adults often find it hard to talk about death too, especially with younger people who they often just want to protect. Some of your closest friends even feel a bit odd about it – maybe they are worried about saying the wrong thing, so they avoid it? It might make them feel awkward or just too sad. Sometimes you might even change the subject yourself, so you can shut it away and pretend it didn't happen. You might just want everything to be *normal* again.

But in this book, no matter what, we are going to talk about what has happened with bravery and honesty. Because the only way to get through this, is by facing it head on. I have a friend called Lee who is an international rugby player. He once told me about something called **courageous conversations**. At the top level of rugby, the players come back after a match and talk openly about the stuff that really matters. I don't know if you watch or play rugby, but a top-class rugby team builds very high levels of **trust** with each other. I always thought it was amazing to watch their speed, their strength and their confidence – how wonderful it must be to be part of a team like that. To become like them you will also need to learn how to be open and talk freely about your feelings to people you trust. You will need to have your own courageous conversations.

I want this book to also become your space to do that – to talk courageously about the stuff that really matters to you. Some of these conversations may well bring tears and others may just leave you feeling drained of energy and a little bit lost; and like the rugby players, we may even have some banter, some happy tears and some genuine laughs.

You may want to read this book alone or maybe there is someone you trust to join us and help with some of the activities. If so, invite them in. Perhaps it could be the person who bought this book for you? They will have bought it because they *care* about you.

The stories from children included in this book are based on the genuine experiences of real people, but names and details have been changed to protect their privacy.

Your memory box

As there will be so many things you will want to treasure along the way, you're going to need somewhere to keep all the special objects and memories safe. So firstly, find a **strong box**. We want it to last a **long** time. Plus, a good **notepad** and a **pencil** or a **pen** to also keep inside your memory box for some of the exercises you may find useful. You may also like to create a **digital part** to the memory box – a great way to store notes, voice recordings, videos and photos.

CHAPTER 1

Why exactly is grief so exhausting?

Dealing with the different emotions that bubble up to the surface when you are experiencing grief can drain your energy, and then figuring out how to live your life now someone important has gone can be very demanding. **Holding on** to the person who has died and at the same time **letting them go** so you can rebuild your life is a bit like trying to pull both ends of a tug of war **at the same time.** You probably have other people around you in your family who are also full of big feelings too.

No wonder it is all so exhausting!

In this chapter I want to show you how important it is to move easily to either side of grief – sometimes you will want to be with your loss to think about the person who has died. At other times you may feel ready to go to the other side – slowly trying to adapt to life without them. So, we will see how both sides can be part of your life – you will never forget and you will find ways to **move on**. First up I would like us to stay on the side of grief where we think a little more deeply about the person who has died. This is the emotional side where feelings usually run high.

Holding on

When you are experiencing grief, it can feel like you don't have control of what's happening. You might find yourself sobbing when you didn't expect tears to come. Or you might have a sudden angry outburst triggered by something small that has nothing to do with the person who has died. For example, going into the kitchen when you are rushing for school only to find there's no cereal left. *'Who ate the last of the cornflakes?!!'* you scream. You slam the door, feel stupid and you struggle to apologise because grief gets in the way, whether you realise it or not. It's somehow easier to get angry about cornflakes than the fact that the person who has died is no longer here. You know how it is. **Nothing is the same**, yet life still goes on. You might start to notice other people's lives in a way you didn't before. *'How come she is moaning about her mum all the time? Doesn't she realise she's so lucky to have a mum?!'*

No wonder it can sometimes be tempting to shut all of your emotions away and never talk about them. Trouble is, if you do this, the grief then gets stuck inside and annoyingly doesn't go away. A girl I know, Zara, described grief to me as feeling like she had a **whole apple stuck in her throat**, which meant she couldn't speak about

her dad's death. In this book we will help you to find good, healthy (and even fun) ways to acknowledge your grief and move forward to rebuild your life. Zara found it a great help to join a group where she met others who totally got it because they had been through the same thing. She is now 23 and can talk about her dad whenever she chooses to with people she trusts.

Another boy I worked with called Jack, whose dad died from a heart attack when he was 13, also said to me, **You have to feel it to heal it.'** Jack also admitted that at first, he found it hard to do this. Thinking about the person who died and how they died is a first step to help with this healing. It makes me smile when I think about how Jack and Zara found their voice and their confidence.

You have to FEEL
IT to HEAL IT.

Campfire stories

On some outdoor adventures, as the night sky gets lit up by the stars and moon, people often light a campfire. It's usually a time when people throw a blanket over their shoulders, relax, feel safe and begin to share stories. As you look into the fire and up to the stars, it can feel natural to share **stories** of our family, our ancestors, people who were important in shaping our lives in some way.

Let's start your own imaginary **campfire conversation**. This might help you to hold on to some important facts about the person who has died. Like lots of important stories, there are probably some parts of the story that are fun and easy to tell and some that are perhaps more difficult and painful. To help get you started, I have suggested some questions (see over the page), but don't be limited by these – this is your relationship, and you know your person best.

Grab your special notebook – we are going to look at some important facts. You will want to keep this information safe in your memory box.

Take your time. Perhaps you can also find a few photos to have in front of you as you think about them. Maybe ask other family members or friends to help you with some of the answers. This will be especially useful if you were very young when your person died. (And it doesn't matter if you cannot answer all of the questions.) Thinking about how they died and how you found out can bring some **strong feelings** to the surface, so be kind to yourself and have a break when you need to.

Here are some questions that might
be useful to think about . . .

What did they look like?
What clothes did they
like to wear?

What were they
good at?

Did they have a
favourite book, film or
piece of music? What
did they watch on TV?

Did anything
make them
frustrated or
angry?

What three words
would you use to
describe them at their
very BEST?

Do you know their date of
birth? Where were they
born? What do you know
about their family? Did
they have any
brothers or sisters?

What might they
choose to have
as a special
meal?

If they were an adult, do you know some of the different jobs they did during their life?

What did they love to do when they were young?

If you could imagine them as an animal, what animal would they be and why?

Is there anything that you particularly liked to do with them?

Did they have a hobby or sport that they enjoyed?

What do you think the highlights of their life were?

If you were buying them a treat, what would it be?

These questions are a bit harder to think about, so be kind to yourself and take breaks from it when you feel you need to.

When did they die?

Do you know how old they were when they died? How old were you?

Do you know yet exactly how they died? (If not, is there someone who can help you understand?)

Where were you on the day they died? Had it been a good day?

When you were told the difficult news, what were you doing and who told you?

41

Well done! What a lot of information you have captured for your **memory box**. Your memory box can act a bit like a time capsule. One day in the future, you may want to look in it again and share your person with people who may not have had the chance to know them. Were there any questions that you couldn't answer yourself? If so, maybe you can think of someone who can help you? Like a journalist, you could interview people who also knew well the person who had died and record their answers. After you have collected your information, you might like to share what you have written or recorded with someone you trust. You may know exactly who to share this with or you might want to think about it.

Are you wondering why I've asked you to begin to tell the story of your time together, when it can be so hard, leaving you feeling a bit sad or drained?

Well, as we have discussed, there are these two sides to grief – one side involves **holding on** to the person who has died and the other is about **letting go** to rebuild your life without them. The exercise you have just completed is all about holding on to important facts – this information will help you think about the person who has died, how they died and to explore the natural emotions of loss that are attached to those memories so you can begin to heal. Remember what Jack told me – you have to feel it to heal it!

But there is also the other side to grief – <u>letting go</u> . . .

The challenge of holding on and letting go

It can be hard to balance holding on and letting go at the same time. To try and get a clear picture in your mind of this challenge – and the idea of grief moving backwards and forwards – let's imagine a rope swing. The swing is attached to a strong branch of a very big tree hanging over a stream. This swing is 100 per cent safe. The tree creates a big canopy of shade on one side of the stream. No flowers grow under the tree on this side, just lovely soft velvety moss. Let's call this space the **land of loss**. Now I want you to imagine that you can jump onto the rope swing and swing safely across the stream and over to the other side. The stream is shallow, warm and slow moving. As you jump off on the other side it's brighter, in full sunshine, and there are flowers growing. Let's call this side the **land of rebuilding**.

Imagine the land of rebuilding represents the place where you can begin to **rebuild your life** after someone has died. This sunny side is about moving on, distracting yourself from some of the painful feelings and trying to deal with all the changes in your life. But sometimes this focus on the future will get too much, so you will want to swing back onto the quiet shaded side – **the land of loss** – where you can relax and simply sob, get furious and scream or just sit with your loss and think quietly about the person who has died.

All your emotions also flow easily in the **land of loss**. When sat here, you might hug the jumper of the person who has died because it still smells like them and it helps you feel close to them. You may find yourself crying or feeling angry. Whereas when you are in the **land of rebuilding** you might want to start clearing out their wardrobe and taking their clothes to a charity shop as you start to slowly rebuild your life. On this side you might also want to set goals, such as doing well at school, fundraising challenges or even practical things like accepting a new person in your house.

When experiencing grief, you may find yourself swinging backwards and forwards on this swing, often several times in the same day, sometimes even in the same hour! In time, you will get comfortable with the **rhythm of grief** as it comes and goes – just like the waves in the sea on the front cover of this book. Eventually you can manage the feelings of loss, together with rebuilding your life. People who study grief call this idea of moving backwards and forwards the DUAL PROCESS (meaning two parts) theory of grief. This is the idea that you zigzag backwards and forwards between feeling your loss and rebuilding your life. It seems to work well for a lot of people, and I hope it makes sense to you. Is your rope swing moving backwards and forwards or do you maybe feel a bit stuck on one side of the stream at times?

When grief gets stuck

Holding on and letting go can still be tricky so you don't get **stuck** on one side of the stream. There's someone very famous from history who found it difficult to get on the imaginary 'grief swing'. You might be very familiar with Queen Victoria. She found the letting go aspect of grief very hard to do and was stuck in the **land of loss.** Prince Albert was her much-adored husband, and he died suddenly when he was just 42. For 40 years (the rest of her life) Queen Victoria dressed in black, often finding it hard to talk to people and appear in public. Certainly at first, it was very difficult for her to both hold on to Albert and to let go and rebuild her life. The holding on part of her grief somehow shut everything else out.

THE LAND OF REBUILDING

However, some people also get stuck in the **land of rebuilding** – they can't bear to think about the person they've lost, so they push their feelings deep down and ignore them. Many people who get too stuck on restoring and rebuilding their life will take on projects so they can be **busy, busy, busy** – often to distract themselves from those painful feelings of loss.

Though finding a balance between holding on and letting go will feel easier, there is no one way to grieve. You will figure out how and when you want to get onto your rope swing.

You may find that you feel people are judging you on how you are doing. Grief is private and often people don't really understand it. We will talk a lot in this book about trying to find someone who you can trust to understand your grief. But in terms of holding on and letting go, you will be the person who will find a healthy **rhythm** of visiting the land of loss and the land of rebuilding. The exercises in this book will help you with both sides of your riverbank so you find the balance that is right for you.

There is a saying:

'Kindness is the key to the kingdom.'

This is a time to be kind to yourself and speak bravely to someone you trust about what has happened. Eventually your feelings of grief will unlock. They will start to feel **less heavy** to carry and your swing can perhaps move backwards and forwards more easily.

A few years ago, I received an invitation to meet the Queen. She wanted to thank me for working with children who had been bereaved, so I was invited to the Palace with lots of other people who she also wanted to thank. I was **excited** but, on the morning, when I looked in the mirror before leaving for Buckingham Palace I started to cry. How strange, I thought to myself. I knew this was a special day to celebrate. I suddenly felt deeply sad that my dad could not be with me. He had died suddenly of a heart attack and, like many of you, we had no chance to say goodbye. I knew that I needed to dip into my grief toolbox quickly. I looked in the cupboard where I keep a **memory box** for my dad and took out an old bottle of his favourite aftershave, Old Spice. It has quite a distinctive smell and when I smell it, I remember being in the bathroom as a little girl watching my dad shave. I splashed it all over my new outfit and me. Quite a lot in fact! Smells can really create a strong connection to our emotions. (The Queen didn't mention my 'interesting' choice of perfume!)

I felt my dad was with me on my special day. I wonder if the young Queen Elizabeth II felt like that on her Coronation in 1953? Her father had died earlier when she was away in Kenya and she didn't get the chance to say goodbye either. She was 25 and went on to be Britain's longest-reigning monarch.

ROALD DAHL

Squishous, squizzle and scrumdiddlyumptious, fizzlecrump and fizzwiggler . . . only a really special storyteller could think up such wonderful words!

Over a hundred years ago in 1920, something very sad happened in the life of a person who went on to become one of the most famous storytellers of the 20th Century.

Roald Dahl was only three years old when his seven-year-old sister Asti died from a burst appendix. In his autobiography Roald Dahl explains that he was literally **speechless** for days after Asti died. Then, only weeks later, his father became sick with an illness called pneumonia and died.

Life changed a lot for the Dahl family after his sister and father died. His mum was expecting a baby when her husband died and a few years later, Roald was sent away to boarding school.

Roald writes about his mother with great affection, and he describes her as a most wonderful storyteller. Much later in life he became a storyteller himself. He wrote lots of books and in them, he always gave the good characters special powers and great values to steer them through **stormy waters**. In his first ever story for children – *James and the Giant Peach* – we learn that James had a lovely life with his parents until he suddenly became an orphan. Both his parents are killed by a rhino coming out of a cloud in the sky! And so, James starts off on his own grief journey but gets through it with gritty determination and friendship. In Roald's amazing book *Matilda*, a little girl finds someone she trusts to help her get through difficult times with her family – a kind teacher called Miss Honey. And in the book *The BFG*, Sophie – also an orphan – and a big friendly giant go on a journey together. Bits of that journey are truly horrible, but other parts are comforting.

Roald's own daughter died of measles when she was seven and he asked for some of the money from his book sales to be given to help children with serious health conditions. He clearly had to cope with much sadness and grief in his own life, but perhaps writing helped him to **make sense** of those feelings.

In many of
Roald Dahl's
stories, the message
is that although things
can get tough,
YOU WILL BE OKAY.

CHAPTER 2

I like to imagine that grief is a bit like one big, hard workout. It's intense, exhausting and frankly after a long day at school, it can be the last thing you want to do. But by doing little exercises, day-by-day, you can slowly strengthen your **grief muscles** – finding easier ways of coping and growing stronger as you do. Now I know what you're thinking, people don't have actual 'grief muscles' in their bodies. You're right, I've made them up! But let's pretend they do exist and that each one of them helps you to grow, stay strong and feel healthy. Once you've developed and really flexed them, even the most difficult days will seem possible to get through. These are the muscles that mean you can jump on your swing several times a day when you need to. That sounds useful doesn't it?

The magnificent seven

Let's get to know these **seven grief muscles** that will help you to be stronger and more hopeful – the metaphorical muscles we're going to be flexing to take you on your grief journey. The muscles that will help you to swing backwards and forwards from the land of loss to the land of rebuilding.

TRUST

Choosing to talk openly with people who want to understand and listen

It is vital that you find a few people that you know are reliable, honest and you feel safe with. It doesn't have to be lots of people. Just a couple of people to help support you, people who won't judge you or mind being asked for help. On pages 67–68 I have added a checklist that may be helpful to show to the people you choose to be your trusted friends. The other benefit of building up the trust muscle is that it helps you to trust yourself.

CONFIDENCE

Being sure of yourself

People are often surprised at how much confidence they lose when someone has died. Where does it go? Before the person died, life was how it was and now life can seem less secure in some ways. Have you noticed that at all? Maybe you have always struggled with your self-confidence and losing someone has made it even harder. Sometimes going back to school can be hard, for example, and you suddenly feel a bit less confident about who you are and what to say to people.

MEMORY

Building a memory store that can comfort and reassure you

Holding on to your important or special memories of the person who has died is important. Sometimes it may feel as though it could be better to forget the person because the memories seem to lead to such sadness, but you will find that managing your memories carefully will become a more and more important part of moving forward.

Selecting the memories that help us to feel good and finding ways to contain any memories that are unhelpful and painful is so helpful. We will talk a lot more about managing all your different memories in chapter 3.

GRIEF MINDSET

Beliefs that help you grow beyond your loss

A mindset is a way that we choose to think about something. If your mindset is healthy, it can help you to maintain a better mood and helps you to grow. When you are grieving it is often not possible to maintain a positive mindset all the time. You definitely need space to feel thoroughly miserable at times. But working to build a strong grief mindset will help you to grow around your loss. For example, sometimes people may have a regret about the way someone died. A grief mindset would help them to accept that they never wanted it to happen this way and that they are not to blame in any way. It's a very important muscle that often takes time to develop, so we will talk lots more about this in chapter 4.

GRIT

Finding your inner strength and looking forward

'Grit' is a great word to say out loud. Have a go – shout it loud. 'I HAVE GRIT!' As the name suggests, this muscle gives you great strength. Strong muscles need perseverance and hard work. With this gutsy determination you'll be more able to handle things. You have grit. This muscle will help you to bounce back when things don't go according to plan. It gives you a resilience (or what some people call, 'bounce-back ability') to follow your dreams. But it takes some work and perseverance to build this muscle. When we meet footballer Sir Bobby Charlton at the end of this chapter, you will see he needed a lot of grit when he returned to playing professional football after a terrible loss. We will also meet a lot of well-known people who have shown a lot of grit in chapter 4.

FLEXIBLE FEELINGS

Showing them, not showing them. Sharing them, not sharing them

This is a very interesting muscle as it helps you to notice, accept and express your feelings AND it also helps you control your emotions when you need to. For example, if I had burst out crying in front of the Queen because I missed my dad it could have been a bit awkward. I am sure she would have coped and may well have had a clean handkerchief in her handbag for me, but I would have probably felt a bit embarrassed. So it was better on that occasion to be able to cry in the mirror in the morning and then have a strong smiley face for the day. This flexible feelings muscle helps you to respect your feelings, control them and importantly NOT lock them away. In other words, it takes guts to cope with the feelings of grief and this muscle helps you to be in control. We will look at this important muscle throughout the book and especially in chapter 5, where we will also look at how others in your family may be showing their feelings.

BALANCE

Finding time to rest and play. Holding onto the past and letting go to rebuild your life

Remember the grief swing and the challenge of holding on and letting go? We know that it's tough keeping everything well balanced when you are grieving – that's why it's so important to move between the land of loss and, at the same time, take a break, move about, make plans and even begin to have fun in the land of rebuilding. Grief requires you to rebalance, as you adjust to different experiences. The other important part of the balance muscle is looking after yourself and others. Grief can feel very heavy, so we need to use this muscle to lighten the load. Looking after yourself and others is necessary as grief can exhaust you. It's important to work, rest and play and we will take a closer look at this in chapter 6.

Now seven is a lot of muscles, and we will look at all of them more closely throughout the book. You will find that you will use them all together and occasionally in isolation. You may find you like some of them more than others, but it is a good idea to try them ALL in order to find out! In this chapter I will concentrate on two. **Trust** and **confidence**.

So first up –
TRUST

The trust muscle

TRUSTED FRIENDS – people you can rely on. You are comfortable talking about the serious stuff with them because you feel safe with them.

Trusted friends can be an adult or people of a similar age who you simply enjoy hanging out with to escape from the weight of grief.

But sometimes you need people to share the more difficult stuff with. Remember earlier we spoke about courageous conversations? Well during your grief journey you're going to have to have a lot of these. It's seriously important to find some good people to have these conversations with. Maybe one or two adults and a good friend your age. Maybe you already have people in mind. Someone you can confidently ask for help because you **trust** them. That could be anyone – a close friend, an aunt or uncle or a teacher that you feel comfortable with and like.

But asking for <u>HELP</u> can be hard.

There is a line in a book by author and illustrator Charlie Mackesy that best sums it up. In it there is a picture of a boy and a horse.

The boy asks the horse, 'What's the **bravest** thing you've ever said?' and the horse replies, **'Help'**.

Going to people and asking for help is not always straightforward, especially if your confidence is low.

But there is a very interesting fact that I want you to know. Quick question:

How do you think MOST people feel MOST of the time when they ask for HELP?

I asked this same question to a group of confident businesspeople and they said:

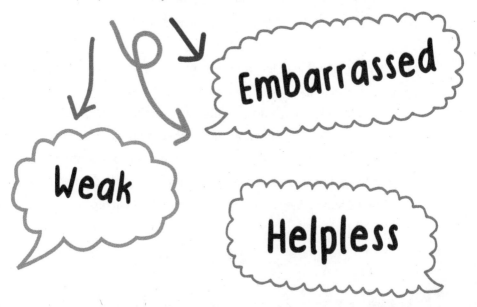

Embarrassed

Weak

Helpless

I then asked them: How do you feel when people ask *you* for help?

They said they felt:

Proud

Trusted

Pleased to be asked

That's interesting, isn't it? All of us (me included) often think twice about asking for help and yet when other people ask us for our help, we can find it a really positive experience, a chance to be a **thinking partner** to help someone to figure out what's bothering them. We are pleased to be asked.

So, are you managing to let trusted people in or are you wanting to keep your grief more locked away? A boy I have worked with called Freddie explained that as he became more familiar with grief, he would imagine putting it away at the bottom of his wardrobe so people couldn't see him feeling upset. Freddie was only eight when his mum died, but was very focussed on being independent and his best friends sometimes didn't know how best to help him.

A few years ago, the people at the **Child Bereavement Network** came up with a great idea. They realised that even trusted friends sometimes struggle to know what to do or say. They created cards for you to show to a friend (and others) so they would know how to help you. I have created a similar one below. You may want to change it and make your own or you could simply show your friend this list and then chat about which ones matter most to you.

Asking for help from a trusted friend

Dear (name of your friend)
_____

As you may know my (name of your person) has died. You are a good friend and I trust you. I have ticked some of the things below that are particularly important to me now. I hope that reading them may make it easier for both of us.

- ✓ Be my friend and be yourself – even if you don't know what to do or say. Just knowing you are there helps
- ☐ Please don't act differently around me
- ☐ Ask me if there's anything you can do if I am having a bad day
- ☐ Give me a hug if I look sad
- ✓ Help me to have fun and laugh sometimes

Ask me if I want to talk about the person who has died, sometimes I do and sometimes I don't

☑ If people keep crowding in and asking me too many questions, can you help me out, so I don't have to talk to everyone about it all the time?

☐ Give me space sometimes, I know you care

☐ If you are worried about me and think I need to go and see someone, talk to me so I can ask where I may be able to find that help

☐ Don't feel you have to do things to please me

☑ When we talk about important topics, I need to know that you won't tell others without asking me

☑ Give me a break if I am acting a bit strangely, having a bad day or being a bit grumpy. I may be upset about something and need to be alone. Please don't get offended. My feelings are all over the place

Please understand that the ones I have ticked are for how I feel now, things may change. Let's chat some more and thank you for reading this – you are a **good friend**.

From _____

I wonder which friend you will show this to first. It works for friends your own age and also for adults such as a trusted teacher or family member. Whatever you do, remember asking for help is a **brave** thing to do and that people feel good when they are asked. They know you are trying to cope with a very big thing in your life. And when things are very big, we all need an extra boost of confidence, support and someone to just be there for us.

HELP!

Asking for help is a
BRAVE thing to do
(and people feel good
when they are asked.)

Let's look at what could
help to build confidence
in this next section.

The confidence muscle

So we now know it is good to have one or two people who properly understand what you are dealing with. This is important because there will be lots of people who may ask you questions that you find a bit awkward. Your trusted friend can help you practise how to cope with these situations with this next exercise.

There is an ancient Chinese saying, 'A journey of a thousand miles starts with a single step.' And in many ways, this is **step one** in building the grief confidence muscle.

The challenge of this first step is to be able to say ...

what has happened

and who has died

in **one short sentence** to people who ask, because they care.

I know this may make some of you gulp. It's that apple in the throat moment. But if you practise, it will help you to say what has happened and to know that you are not going to feel overwhelmed by your emotions when someone asks. You can practise this sentence in a mirror (or with your trusted friend) saying it **over and over again**. Awkward questions will begin to feel less awkward. Eventually you will simply reply with confidence. But at first you may feel a bit wobbly inside and you may even have to take a deep breath halfway through your reply if you feel your voice breaking or tears welling up.

Here are the experiences of four young people who really started to build their confidence muscle by getting their **grief sentence** sorted and ready to use.

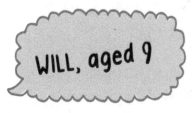

WILL, aged 9

Let me first share Will's story. He was nine when his grandad died suddenly in a car accident. Will's grandad was super important in his life. They did everything together. He also picked him up from school each day. After his grandad died, Will was off school for the funeral. When he returned, someone at the school gate – a cheerful but concerned mother of one of Will's friends – said, 'Is your grandad late today Will? That's unusual, isn't it?'

When she said this, Will's heart sank. He looked away and wanted to disappear. He couldn't talk about it as he was worried he might cry in front of everyone.

What did Will say? Did he say nothing? Did he lie and say 'my grandad will be here soon'?

NO. Will took a deep breath, and confidently said:

'You may not have heard, but Pops died in a car accident two weeks ago in half term. Thanks for asking. I need to go now as my mum will be here soon.'

The **confidence muscle** kicked in and helped Will get a short sentence out without feeling too emotional. His mum had helped him practise it. Will ran off quickly afterwards as he didn't want to risk having a longer chat, but he was proud to have said it. And the next day when someone else asked, it was a tiny bit easier.

So, do you get the idea? What we are looking for is a sentence that you have practised that will give you **confidence** in the moment should someone who cares about you ask. Just a short, simple sentence that is said with warmth but allows you to escape when you've had enough.

EMMA, aged 15

Emma was 15 when her brother died from a long illness. She had been his carer alongside others in the family. They had known since Sam was born that he could die at any moment. When that moment finally came, she found it very tough. Emma would simply say to people:

'We are heartbroken that Sam has died. It was such a long, difficult illness, and he was incredibly brave, but we are pleased that he died peacefully in the hospice and without any pain.'

SARINA, aged 12

Some stories are of course even more complicated and you may not choose to say exactly how your person died, especially to someone you don't know very well. Sarina, who was 12, had to think about her confident one-liner sentence carefully. Her dad had died from drinking alcohol very heavily. It was a complicated story and her dad had often been angry and occasionally violent. At times, Sarina found it **hard** to say she loved him (she really didn't like his rages) and felt angry when people assumed that her dad was a 'brilliant' man. Sarina was naturally struggling with lots of difficult feelings; however, she decided she would say:

'Thanks for asking, my dad died very suddenly in October last year. It's been a tough year for us as a family, but we are supporting each other. Must go now . . .'

She only told the more detailed story to people she really trusted.

So, you see, every story is different, and everyone will have a different way of talking about what has happened.

Time now to figure out your one-liner. Write it in your notebook or record it on your phone and practise saying it over and over, out loud. Once you have really learned this sentence it means you can say it on the good days and also on days when your mood may be lower and you feel a little more wobbly.

Remember, it's okay not to tell people everything – it's only with people you really trust that you will feel comfortable sharing the full story.

So, you see, by beginning to train just two of your grief muscles – **CONFIDENCE** and **TRUST** – you are finding strength. You may not always feel ready to open up completely; however, when you do, your reply is now sorted. It's a good place to start, having a conversation about the person who has died, trusting other people and navigating some situations you might find a bit, well awkward. The more you do this, the stronger you will get. Let's now hear about a footballer who very suddenly needed to build up his grief muscles.

SIR BOBBY CHARLTON

Sir Bobby Charlton is regarded as one of the greatest English football players of all time. Bobby was a member of the England team that won the 1966 FIFA World Cup against Germany. (The first and only time England has ever won – at the time I am writing!)

However, the story I want to tell you takes place eight years before that famous World Cup win. Bobby played almost all his club football at the same club – **Manchester United**. The strategy in those days was to grow talent rather than buy it. So the manager (Sir Matt Busby) needed to scout for teenage lads who looked like they had the right skills.

In 1958 Bobby Charlton was one of those young lads. Belonging to this team meant the world to Bobby, a shy 20-year-old who simply loved football.

He joined the club at 17 and it had taken him three years to finally get chosen to play with all his friends in the **first team**. He was delighted to have played well in a big match against the Red Stars in Belgrade. Although the weather was very bad, the team were in a celebratory mood as they boarded a plane in Munich, Germany to make the final stage of their journey back home to Manchester.

It was February and it had started to snow and rain heavily. There were 44 passengers on this small plane and the passengers included all 11 members of the first team.

Tragically the pilot ran out of runway on take-off and the plane crashed into a house. It burst into flames. The goalkeeper pulled Bobby from the wreckage and he miraculously escaped without any injuries. However, eight of his good friends and fellow team players died that night, along with 15 other passengers.

Bobby was consumed with grief and he said some years later,

'Life was never the same, suddenly all my pals were missing . . . it was a very traumatic time for the club.'

He was a survivor and his friends had died. Initially he talked about feeling guilty because he survived and his friends didn't, and how he would ever play again. It took a while as he had very strong feelings of intense loss that were hard to express because of the trauma of the crash. However, Bobby was known for having true **grit**. He slowly began to trust in his new teammates and eventually that **grief mindset** really took hold. He started to believe that he could grow beyond this terrible loss and he returned to play professional football, working relentlessly hard. Even though at times it must have been painful, Bobby spoke regularly about his eight teammates and friends who died that night. He had the energy to allow his grief swing to be powered backwards and also forwards as the team rebuilt itself.

Forty years later, Bobby proudly led the Manchester United team up the stairs to receive their third European Cup. That match was dedicated to the 23 people who died in the Munich plane crash in 1958. Bobby held on to the emotions and memories of his lost friends, but he also managed to let go, rebuild a football team and, in doing so, he did his teammates proud. In his older years he would often turn up and play with the youth teams. Maybe they reminded him of himself at the beginning of his career?

What an incredible man.

CHAPTER 3

We all have memories, and memories can trigger different types of emotions. Some memories spark **joy**, but others can be sad or more **awkward** or painful. There are those happy events we remember such as midnight feasts, camping with friends, and then there are more difficult memories like being stung by a bee and falling off your bike into a bush.

It's the same when it comes to remembering the person who has died. As you now know, memories are important for the 'holding on' part of grief. But our memories are not all the same. There are some **grief memories** that are comforting, and you will want to hold on to these kinds of memories forever. And there may be other memories that are a bit distressing or even traumatic, and we need to find a way to acknowledge them and eventually shrink them, to make them more manageable.

The memory muscle

Have a quick think – how much time do you spend on memories of the person that died that spark joy and smiles and how much time do you spend on memories that are more difficult and leave you feeling unhappy? On your grief journey I will help you to find ways to dilute the power of those more difficult memories. One way to do this is just by talking! Simply talking about sad memories to someone you trust can massively decrease their power. But there are also other things you can do to flex your **memory muscle** in a positive way.

Some memories spark joy, but others can be sad or more awkward or painful.

Three memory stones

One way of balancing different types of memories is to select three different stones and imagine these are your 'memory stones'. One will be a rough rock, one will be a round pebble and the other will be a gemstone or something a little more attractive than the others. Each stone represents different types of memories.

Let's start with the easy one – the **PEBBLE**. The simple pebble is ordinary – a smooth, rounded stone that is easy to hold. There are probably lots of them out in the park or garden. This stone represents the ordinary, everyday comforting memories about the person who has died.

Find a smooth pebble and start to make a list of your everyday pebble memories in your notebook. To give you an idea here's some pebble-type memories that I've heard others say:

✳ We loved walking the dog up the hill each morning.

✳ She would have a sliced banana on her porridge every day.

* We always watched the *Toy Story* films together.

* His jumper smelled of soap and engine oil when he came home from work.

* She was terrible at cooking – once she left a roast chicken in the oven for a week!

* Grandma and I loved learning new Bhangra Boogie Dance routines together. She was so active!

The second stone is very different from the simple, smooth pebble. The little, rough **ROCK** feels sharp and painful when you hold it tightly. Look for a small rock that has jagged edges. This rock represents the **harder times** and also maybe some particular memories of the way the person died that may make you shudder.

Here are some rocky memories that others have shared with me:

* I went away camping with Scouts on the day she died – she had been ill for so long. I promised myself I would be there when she died.

* I didn't get to say goodbye when he died from the virus in hospital – he was all alone.

* Grandad was in a home and he didn't even know me any more.

* She had a terrible temper, so we would hide in the cupboard.

He was always shouting at me to tidy my room, get my hair cut and finish my homework. I am messy, but I didn't mean to upset him.

 I had a big row with her just before the accident happened. I said things that were unkind. Things I didn't actually mean.

You can see this rough rock represents some exceptionally **tough** types of memories. It may be that you have none of these kinds of memories. However, if you do have some difficult memories that are painful like this, please do tell someone you trust. It's okay to ask for help. In fact, we now know it's **brave** to ask for help. You are at your grittiest self when you notice these tough memories and decide to do something about them. Later in the book, we have a section on the toughest types of memories (pages 143-6). We call these **traumatic memories** and they often need professional help, so it's good to notice them and ask for some help.

Despite not being easy, your rough rock still has a place in your bag of memory stones. It's important to recognise how you have coped with the difficult memories that may have been part of your life. You will learn to talk and manage those memories so they can't overshadow the memories that bring joy, comfort and smiles. Talking of joy . . .

There's one more stone to include.

The third stone is a colourful <u>GEMSTONE</u>.

The gemstone is there to remind you to hold on to all the **special memories** and **good times** together. These memories may be triggered by lots of things – photos, music, a moment when you both found yourself laughing. We need to hold tight to the memories that make us smile even if they bring on happy tears. They are very specific and it's really important to collect as many of these gemstone memories as possible for your **memory box**. One day you may want to tell people all about them, so you may also need to ask lots of people to help you to record these special moments. Sometimes people who knew the person who died will have stories that you may not know about, so cast your net widely to collect these precious memories. Become a **grief journalist** to make sure you have a digital or written record for now and always.

 Now this is a stone you are very unlikely to find outside. So, you will need to buy it with your money, or you could paint a pebble a bright colour. My favourite gemstones are malachite, lapis lazuli and rainbow moonstone – I wonder, which one will you choose? Whichever you decide on, when you hold it in your hand, it will be a signal to remind yourself of special memories.

Some special gemstone memories I've heard include:

✳ Our holiday. It was such fun canoeing. Mum was silly, and we went round and round in circles before she finally fell in!

The day school was closed because of heavy snow. We made snow angels, watched *Incredibles 2* together and had really delicious hot chocolate.

 My grandad could do handstands until he was 75 – he was so fit, he would race me and let me win.

 My brother was fantastic on drums – he would laugh as I danced around the room with my disco ball while he practised playing.

* Dad loved watching me swim. He would get up really early most mornings to take me to train at the pool. He was there when I got my first silver medal.

Do you have a few **gemstone memories** already? Can you think of some people who also knew your person and who may be able to add more special memories to your memory box? I still carry a little bag of memory stones with me in my backpack and if I am having a difficult day, I get them out in the palm of my hand and remind myself to not only think about difficult memories. When you are feeling down, get your stones out and think about the memories that make you smile.

As well as your memory stones and notes of your special memories – what other things can you keep in your **memory box** that may make you smile and help you to feel connected to the person who has died?

Here are some ideas:

* A card or letter or little message

* Maybe something they wrote for you

* Some video footage that you can edit and store somewhere safe

* A bottle of their perfume or aftershave

* A soft jumper or scarf of theirs to snuggle

* Photos. Lots and Lots. Especially photos of you both together

* Jewellery: a watch or other small objects that remind you of something important

* Something that belonged to them that you love and are allowed to keep in your box

A girl I know called Livvi read out loud a letter her mum had left for her when she knew she was likely to die. Livvi said with a smile and with tears rolling down, 'actually I like it - these are **happy tears**'. I guess it helped her to feel close and reduced her fear that she would somehow forget important memories of her mum. Even if it makes you miss them, it is good to know you're holding on to these special times.

You can also get crafty and make things – you can always ask family or friends to help you with this. Adil was given a lovely soft pillow made from his grandad's T-shirts that he kept in his bed, slightly hidden under his normal pillow. **Holding on** to memories is an important and enjoyable part of making your memory box become a priceless treasure.

Dates to remember

We've looked at past memories, now we're going to look at how we can make **new memories** and still involve the person who has died. To explain the importance of doing this, I am going to talk about two Harrys.

The first Harry is the grandson of Queen Elizabeth II. His mother, Princess Diana, died when **Prince Harry** was 12. It was very important to Prince Harry when he was planning his wedding to involve his mother's memory in lots of lovely ways. He put a lot of thought into creating gemstone memories. Harry and his wife-to-be, Meghan, arranged for the wedding flowers to be picked from Princess Diana's former garden. Prince Harry asked that they play a hymn that was also played at his mother's funeral. Meghan wore a beautiful aquamarine ring that belonged to his mother. Prince Harry was **holding on** and **letting go** in his own way. He figured out how to move forward with his life while still connecting to his past. Sometimes, on big celebratory days like weddings, we ask ourselves 'Am I allowed to be happy if they are not here?'.

Of course, you are! That is exactly what they would have wanted. To hold on **and** to let go **and** to have fun.

Let's think about another Harry who also lost people in his childhood.

Understandable desire

Have you read the Harry Potter books or watched the films?

In the first book, *Harry Potter and the Philosopher's Stone*, we discover that a young wizard called Harry has a strong desire to see his parents. Harry is an orphan – his parents were killed when he was just one, which is particularly tough. He discovers the mirror of **ERISED**. This is **DESIRE** spelt backwards.

Dumbledore, the headmaster of Harry's school, understands Harry's longing to see his parents. His desire to have memories and to see them hurts. Every day it hurts. Dumbledore gently suggests to Harry that he must not dwell only on the past or he may forget to live fully in the present. Perhaps Dumbledore wanted Harry to be able to swing from the **land of loss** to the **land of rebuilding**.

If you have seen the film or read the book you may remember that moment when Harry looks in the mirror of Erised and sees his parents for the first time since they died. It was both amazing and heartbreaking to witness.

Do you also have a desire to see your person one more time? To hold, hug and touch them? This longing is especially hard on important dates when we wish they could be with us.

We may not have the powers to be able to create a magical Mirror of Erised, but it is useful to create a list of your own diary of **dates to remember**. These may be dates when we simply miss the person who has died, for example the day they died, their birthday, your birthday. Then there are the **big** special dates that may only happen now and again – big celebratory days such as weddings – where you might want to figure out how to involve them and how to also have fun.

Prince Harry's brother, **Prince William**, is keeping the memory of his mother, Princess Diana, alive with his children on Mother's Day. His three children create drawings and write letters to their 'granny Diana' for William to mark Mother's Day. Even though she died before they were born, William has made his mother a part of their life too, carrying the memory forward in a comforting way.

Important dates:

* The date they died (this is called the anniversary of their death)

* Birthdays

* Learning a new skill or getting into a new club

* Holidays and day trips

* Religious celebrations

* A new baby arriving in the family

* Your achievements – for example passing some exams, moving to secondary school

* A special family celebration such as a wedding or a graduation

What kind of dates could be important to you, but are hard without the person who has died? Grab your notebook or phone diary and make a note of all the dates next year that are important.

What other dates could be particularly important that are missing from the above list? Ask your family and friends, as they may be already thinking about dates that they are slightly dreading without the person who has died. Together you need a plan so you can help each other cope well on these dates.

Here are three ideas that you may want to discuss with your family or friends to mark important dates.

✳ Light a candle

Perhaps ask an adult to help you choose a special candle, maybe with a lovely scent, that you can light on important dates. Some people light a candle next to a photo (or photos) of the person who has died. **Practical point**: please light any candle safely with an adult to supervise, hair tied back and away from the flame and do not ever leave the candle unattended in a room.

✳ An opportunity to say a few words

Some people like to make a little speech on special occasions and toast 'absent friends'. This is a term for people who have died, raising a glass of something special. It's a public way of taking a moment to say you miss them not being there before you move on and celebrate the occasion.

✳ Take on a fundraising challenge

It could be something that is fun and energetic, easy or hard.
Whatever feels right for you. You may also want to let people know
so that they can support you in raising some money for a charity
you care about, or one that was important to your person.

Tyler Westlake was swept off the rocks by a wave while fishing with friends. **They were totally devastated by his death**. Four months later, they decided to say thank you to the people who searched for him for 48 hours. They arranged a 24-hour gaming marathon to raise funds for the RNLI (Royal National Lifeboat Institution). The friends decided to call their group 'The T Boys' after their best friend Tyler. They all loved the sea, surfing and fishing and said they will miss their evenings playing games together. Their fundraising marathon gaming event was therefore a great connection to their time together and a way of saying **thank you** to the charity that is dedicated to sea rescue and safety.

So far, we have looked at the many ways you can hold on to memories and create what grief specialists call a **continuing connection** or bond with the person who has died.

Simple ideas like those above will be a way to stay connected, especially on dates when you think the world has just moved on and you are here alone and missing them.

Even when someone is no longer able to be by your side, they can be in your **heart**. You **can** take them with you.

People <u>live</u> on in the lives of people who <u>loved</u> them.

Beyond the rough rock
Rebuilding your life after a death by suicide

Every day in the UK, eight children are bereaved of a parent by suicide. Suicide is when someone takes their own life. *Beyond the Rough Rock* is the title of a book that bereavement charity Winston's Wish wrote to help families make sense of a death that can be particularly painful. To explain a little more about this type of grief, I want to introduce you to two people who have worked hard using all their different **grief muscles** to help their jagged painful rock not dominate their other memories of their fathers who both died by suicide. Let's meet Ruben and Dawn.

Ruben

Ruben was three when his father took his own life.
I talked to him 35 years later to see what he had found
particularly hard as a child and he explained:

'As I was growing up, suicide wasn't really talked about
and it took me a while to understand what had happened.
Even at a young age I felt "different" and knew it was something
not easy to talk about. At first I thought that maybe my dad didn't
love me or perhaps I had done something wrong. I was ashamed.
Shame takes a while to shake off. Eventually, when I was about
eight, I was brave enough to ask. My mum and sisters were so

good, they helped me to see that his death wasn't about me. Dad had become mentally unwell and there were other things that didn't help. It took a long time for me to see that it was no one's fault. Not mine, not his, not anyone's. Just lots of sad stuff that was so shocking and took us all a long time to make sense of. We stopped asking "why" and now focus on easier memories and the good times.'

Ruben can now think about his dad more easily and can explain his story to people he trusts, but for most people, he simply says 'my dad died suddenly when I was three, so it was very difficult for our family.'

It takes a lot of **courage** and **practice** of the grief mindset muscle for families to be able to talk openly about suicide. There can be blame, shame and anger with each other and sometimes with the person who has died. When a death is particularly complicated, as with suicide or murder, young people often prefer to meet others in a group who have been through the same kind of death. It can really help both you and others to go forward. Staff at the helplines at the back of this book will be able to talk to you about your situation and suggest some next steps to take.

Dawn French

You may know Dawn, she is a comedy actor and author. She has the **warmest smile** and can be very cheeky. Dawn loved playing the portrait of the Fat Lady in one of the Harry Potter films. She has always had the ability to laugh at herself and creates wonderfully funny characters such as the jolly vicar in the *Vicar of Dibley*.

Dawn also knows first-hand how people who die in our childhood can go on to shape our lives. When she was growing up, she sometimes felt she didn't quite look the same as all the other girls who seemed to get more attention. She talks about how her father was sensitive to her feelings and wanted to ensure she would never lack confidence. In her autobiography she remembers his remarkable words of kindness in her early teenage years that she will **never** forget. 'He sat me down and told me that I was beautiful, that I was the most precious thing in his life, and that he was proud to be my father.'

However, six years later, when Dawn was just a teenager, her father died suddenly. She had been protected from the fact that her father had struggled for a long time with deep depression. The illness finally took over and he quietly died in his car while inhaling carbon monoxide. We call this type of death a suicide. People sometimes describe the grief from a suicide as a *special scar* - a scar that takes a long time to stop being so painful.

As an adult, Dawn also became a successful author. In her first book she decided to write about her life and she wrote it as a series of letters to people who were important in her life. Not surprisingly the first letter in the book was to her dad.

'So, you're still dead. It's been 31 years and every day I have to remind myself of that fact, and every day I am shocked ... I'm not 19 anymore Dad and so many things have happened that you haven't known so I have decided to write this book for you. I wanted to remember our times together and I want to tell you about lots of stuff since. So far it's been better than expected ...'

You can see how Dawn has now **balanced** her three memory stones – she has made lots of space for observing the funny things that happen every day and those really special memories that mean so much. She wants to share them all with her dad and her book is her way to do that.

I hope that, in time, you too will find a way to allow all the memories that you have to sit comfortably together. The 'rocks' have their place in your story, but it's important they don't take over your entire memory space. It's also important to have the confidence to **love yourself** in the powerful way that Dawn and Ruben learned to do. You could even start keeping a diary or just chat to your person out loud, so that you can keep them updated about all the important things that are happening in your life.

CHAPTER 4

We've flexed the trust muscle, honed the confidence muscle, and built the memory muscle – now it's time to think about two other important muscles: the **grit** and the **grief mindset** muscles. These will help you become **the boss of loss**.

Since the person in your life died there may be lots of things that are now on your radar. Things that previously you may not have even noticed. Simple things that you once took for granted. Things that now may cause you to worry. When we grieve, our mind starts working overtime and starts to ask all sorts of questions that are often impossible to answer. These can be relatively small things such as, 'What if I forget to pack my gym kit on Wednesday?' or 'What if I left the front door unlocked?' to much bigger worries such as, 'What if someone else dies?', 'What if I start to cry in school when I don't want to?' or 'What if the gang start on me again?'

The truth is, grief can be both an **energy giver** and an **energy drainer**, depending on how you think about it.

The grief mindset muscle

We know that grief is exhausting so we need to find good ways to help you preserve your energy. Let's start by simply trying to help you catch those worries and help you to become much more aware of spotting the thoughts that drain your energy. They are not nice feelings; they also reduce your confidence and ability to trust people. But positive thoughts increase trust and can leave you feeling so much stronger.

It's a fact. How we <u>think</u> affects how we <u>feel,</u> and that affects how we <u>behave.</u>

Let me give you a quick example of how these thoughts and feelings can often **spiral** out of control, leaving you feeling isolated and lost. Then we'll take a look at how you can approach those thoughts and feelings from a different, more positive perspective. By doing this, although you are dealing with exactly the same situation, you have the tools to deal with it in a way that makes **you** the boss, not your emotions!

Imagine it has been three weeks since your person has died and for most of that time you have stayed indoors. For the first time you've just gone out for a walk with your dog. In the distance on the other side of the road, you see two friends laughing and joking about something, as usual your friends are in hysterics. However, today they just walk by.

Imagine this is what happens in your head:

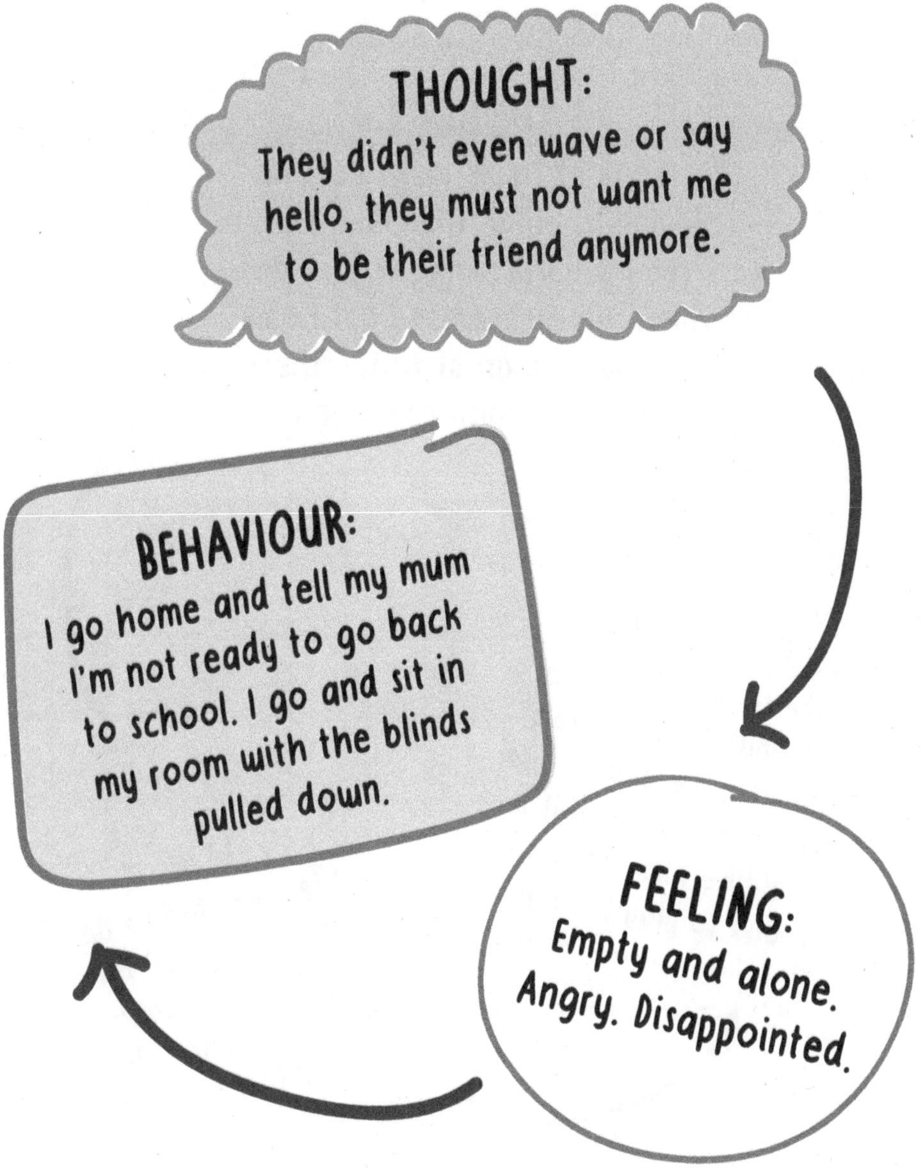

Now let's switch things around. The same thing has happened but this time you're going to think about it a little differently. Ready?

THOUGHT:
Look at them, laughing and joking as usual. They didn't even see me. I will walk the dog and message them when I get home. It would be great to see them. I could do with cheering up.

FEELING:
I feel excited to be back in touch with my friends. To play games and have a kick about would feel so good.

BEHAVIOUR:
I messaged them, they responded immediately. They were pleased to hear from me and asked if it would be okay to come round to play tonight.

Grif vs grief

Do you see how your brain can approach the exact same situation in two different ways? One starts with a **negative thought**, and the other is **more positive**. The thought can completely alter the way that you then feel and how you behave. It's amazing isn't it? By just concentrating on the way you approach something and look at it from a different, more positive perspective, you can feel so much better about something that might otherwise have left you feeling really sad.

But we all have negative thoughts sometimes, and it can be harder to deal with them when you're grieving. These negative thoughts are the ones that seem to gobble up your energy and really affect your mood. They can leave you feeling **hopeless** and **lost**. When it comes to grief, I like to imagine this **energy sucker** is **Grif**, a greedy goblin of grief. Grif wants you to have destructive feelings that make you feel empty and low in energy.

Grif will steal your energy.

Grif thinking creeps in when your mood is low. When you're tired and fed up. Its purpose is to make you have difficult thoughts that lead to heavy feelings, so you feel bad about yourself and others. Grif thinking is very fixed, unlike you who are usually more open and curious. But we're about to discover how you can notice Grif thinking and manage it.

What's the essential difference between **Grif** and **Grief?**

Yes! You are right – just one letter, **E!**

E for Energy

Grif thinking is an **energy-sucker**, an energy-hoover. It wants to leave you feeling empty and steal your energy. His unhelpful way of thinking needs to be spotted, captured, and put in a box allowing you the space to train and fully flex your **grief mindset**. The mindset that helps you to face forward with more energy and hope.

Let me show you how we can get better at having a **Grif radar**. Take a look at the thoughts on the pages that follow and imagine how different you might feel if you followed the grief mindset thoughts and beliefs compared to the Grif way of thinking.

Grif thinking

Grandad has died, life is now bad, family life will NEVER be the same ~~or quite as good.~~

Grief mindset

Life has changed a lot since grandad died. We are trying hard to support each other and have some good times together.

Grif thinking

What if mum meets someone and they move in together? I don't want a new dad or new brothers and sisters. That would be dreadful.

Grief mindset

If mum did meet someone, they wouldn't replace my dad. I would try hard to get to know them and talk to mum about it. My school and friends are important to me right now, so I need mum to understand that I don't want to move.

Grif thinking

I am terrified that I will cry about my friend in front of my classmates. They will think I am stupid and weak.

Grief mindset

If I did cry in front of my friends it's not the end of the world. They know it's natural and I know that when I cry in public, my tears don't last that long.

Grif thinking

Everyone else is in happy families except me. I hate watching those happy-family Christmas adverts on TV. Now it's just mum and me. She has to work two jobs. No one understands how much I miss my grandma.

Grief mindset

My grandma was very special to me. She helped me so much when things were difficult after dad left and mum needed to be away with her work. Maybe I need to explain to my friends a bit more about why her death has affected me so much.

Grif thinking

Mum asked me what I wanted to do to think about him on his birthday. I said 'nothing'. Why does she MAKE me talk about him? I hate these feelings. I hate the fact that he's not here.

Grief mindset

I knew I would miss my brother on his birthday. Mum and I discussed it - we said we would have his favourite meal (burger and chips) and light a candle. I miss him. I know Mum does too. He was a great brother, we argued lots and I still miss him loads.

Do you get the idea? Are you noticing how negative Grif thinks and on the other hand what a more hard-working, positive grief mindset can think and then feel like?

Grif thinking sucks on your energy and is often draining, affecting both your confidence and enthusiasm.

A **grief mindset**, on the other hand, can help you to have the energy to face the future and hold onto beliefs that will strengthen you. It keeps the boat in the storm pointing in the best direction towards calmer waters. You are growing with your grief rather than being exhausted and overwhelmed by it.

You may find it helpful to meet other children who are going through grief too. When you get a chance to chat to others, you will quickly see that everyone struggles to get on top of this energy-draining thinking after someone has died. Young people have always told me that meeting others in a similar situation helps a lot. It builds your **confidence** as you know there is no treading on eggshells – you are all in the same spot, finding your way forward.

Ask an adult to call the helplines at the end of the book to help you find ways to meet others who may have experienced a similar type of death. There may even be people in your school that have been bereaved who you could chat to – you could ask your teacher if they can find out for you.

Grief can feel like a
stormy ocean that
you are trying to navigate
in a small boat . . .
but just as in nature,
all storms
eventually pass.

Kinder thinking

Now it's time to keep building those **confidence muscles** – you can start by being kinder to yourself.

One of the phrases people say a lot is **if only I . . .** When they say this little phrase, they feel guilt or have a sense of shame. Shame and guilt are unkind, energy-draining emotions – both are deeply unhelpful and not surprisingly, they belong to Grif thinking.

Take a moment and think of your **if onlys.** They could be something like:

✳ IF ONLY I had told them not to work so hard

✳ IF ONLY I had noticed that she was unwell

✳ IF ONLY I hadn't made her late for that meeting

✳ IF ONLY I had called the ambulance right away and it had arrived sooner

✳ IF ONLY I knew that he was in such a violent gang

Can you see how these thoughts are negative? By thinking in this way, it makes you feel like you are somehow to blame, even though you never intended them to die. When you notice these thoughts it's good to talk them through with someone. **Healthy grief** allows you to talk openly about any regrets that you may have and move forward. Remember, be kind to yourself and don't punish yourself with draining thoughts.

Shoulds are just as tough ...

Have you noticed that each time you say the word **should** it is as if you are quietly telling yourself off? Saying 'I should' does not help you to feel confident. It sounds a little bit like you are not good enough.

✳ I SHOULD get good marks in my exams, it's bad to disappoint people

✳ I SHOULD stop losing my temper

✳ I SHOULD go to the concert

✳ I SHOULD go visit the grave with mum

119

The thinking trick with a **should** is to convert it to a **could** and then make a positive **plan**. This stops you telling yourself off and feeling bad. It is a small change that can have a positive effect on your confidence levels.

✳ I COULD get good marks in my exam, so I am going to start a revision plan today

✳ I COULD stop losing my temper; I will need to have a chat with mum, so she knows how I feel

✳ I COULD go to the concert; however, I really don't want to, so I am going to let Kate know that I am going to stay at home and read my book

✳ I COULD go to the grave with mum, but I feel closer to dad listening to the music we both liked. I will explain this to mum rather than keep making excuses

Can you see how this type of healthy grief mindset thinking is **kinder** to yourself and others? When you are grieving, it helps to be kind and not judge yourself (or others) too harshly. The feelings you are having are natural, so the last thing you need is a critical voice in your head. When you are hurting, things are more sensitive than usual, so **practise kindness** on yourself. It is important as it will also help you to soften those strong waves of grief. We can't control what happens to us, but we can control **how we respond**. Count to five, take some deep breaths and think about how you want other people to feel about you after you have left the room. Maybe others in your family or friendship group will notice and you can all be kinder to each other as a result.

By building your **grief mindset** muscle, you can experiment with thinking in a more courageous way, you can start to make decisions to enjoy life again and gradually to feel more in control of how you think, feel and behave. It takes time, but it is a skill that will last you all your life.

The grit muscle

Another great approach to help you look forward is the **grit muscle**. Grief can be very overwhelming but it's surprising how 'battling with grief' can leave you feeling stronger and more determined than before you were bereaved.

You may have heard of the famous inventor **James Dyson**. When he was nine, he started at the boarding school his father taught at, but not long after he joined the school, his father died. At school, in his early teens, James took up long-distance running. Many people who have been bereaved talk about how running helps. James built up a mental strength and grit that also helped him later in life at work. He is now one of the most successful people in business. However, it was not an easy path to success at all. It took him 5,126 different versions of a vacuum cleaner before he finally got it right! Yes ... that's 5,126 failures. He flexed his **grit muscle**, learnt from his mistakes and over 15 long years was determined and proud to design inventions that have changed the world.

Eddie Izzard is a stand-up comedian, a writer, an actor and a political activist who tries to gather people around a goal and set big challenges. Eddie is also someone who has experienced grief.

When she was five, her mum died and she was sent to boarding school at six years old. In 2021, she set a New Year's Fundraising Challenge – her most ambitious to date. She called it a Run for Hope and set herself the goal of running 31 marathons in the 31 days of January - followed by performing a live comedy show each evening! Eddie's ambition and slogan is, *'to make humanity great again'*. All the money raised from the challenge will go to charities that work towards a better, fairer and kinder world. She said that even when we feel exhausted, we can all do more than we think we can. That's her **grit muscle** working so hard for a great purpose.

I think so many young people that I have met seem to show tremendous **grit** after someone in their lives has died. In the stories that follow, we can see a little more how the saying 'what doesn't break you makes you stronger' has played out in the lives of leaders whose own lives were very much shaped by the experience of early loss.

Bosses of loss

It might surprise you to know that there are a lot of experts, businesspeople and world leaders who were bereaved when they were young. Many of them do say that they had dark and lonely times, yet their grief also pushed them to pursue their dreams and goals and, surprisingly, gave them more determination to succeed.

Here are just a few of them:

Nelson Mandela

Many people respect and admire this man. He was a civil rights leader and President of South Africa. Earlier in his life, Mandela was unfairly imprisoned on an island for 27 years for protesting against apartheid – a political system in South Africa where non-white citizens were segregated (kept apart) from white people and did not have equal rights. Mandela was only nine years old when his father died. He said,

'I defined myself through my father ... he had a proud rebelliousness, a stubborn sense of fairness and I recognise myself in that.'

When Mandela left prison, he could have behaved like an angry victim of a great injustice, but he chose not to. Mandela's mindset is respected by people all over the world. His values established as a child shaped how he chose to lead himself and his people.

He had the most amazing grief mindset and grit. He powerfully and peacefully showed great leadership, won the Nobel Prize for Peace and South Africa was liberated from apartheid.

Justice Ruth Bader Ginsberg

Ruth was a very courageous and gutsy leader who worked for 27 years in the Supreme Court of the United States (the highest court in the USA). Ruth often said how her mother's words guided her throughout her life and especially when she faced big injustices in the world.

> 'My mother told me to be a lady. And for her, that meant be your own person. Be independent.'

Her mother died from cancer when Ruth was graduating from school and her sister died from meningitis when Ruth was just six years old. She was known to have a lot of **grit**. How did this tiny, shy, yet superstrong and determined woman from Brooklyn get to be known by young people as the **Notorious RBG**? Justice Ginsberg found her nickname funny. Young people look to her as a role model in working hard for what you believe in. She would say try not to argue with everyone, but pick the important battles wisely.

Joe Biden

Did you know that one in three American presidents had a parent die when they were young? George Washington, Thomas Jefferson, Herbert Hoover, Gerald Ford, Bill Clinton and Barack Obama all lost their fathers while they were young. The President of the United States, Joe Biden, has also had to cope with tremendous grief in his life.

Joe's first wife and baby daughter were killed in a car crash in 1977. Then in 2015, his eldest son Beau died from a brain tumour. After his son's death, President Biden wrote a very uplifting biography called *Promise Me, Dad: A Year of Hope, Hardship and Purpose.* 'Promise me' is one of those little phrases that people remember so vividly to help them through their grief when someone dies. Before he died, Beau asked his father:

'Promise me, Dad, give me your word that no matter what happens, you're going to be alright?'

Joe Biden gave his son his word. He became the 46th President of the United States five years after Beau died. The night before he was made President, Joe gave a speech about his son and tears rolled down his face as he spoke – that night he was comfortably in the **land of loss** and the next day ready for his inauguration – the **land of rebuilding**.

Sir Winston Churchill

Sir Winston Churchill (prime minister of the United Kingdom between 1940-45 and 1951-55) had a difficult relationship with his parents, especially his father, who was said to have had a very bad temper. Despite this, as a child Churchill worshipped his father and was always seeking his **praise**, wanting to make him **proud**.

Randolph Churchill died when Winston was young. Later in his life, Winston requested that when he himself died, he would be buried next to his father in a small cemetery in Oxfordshire, instead of in Westminster Abbey like eight other prime ministers before him and 17 British kings and queens! He wanted to be close to his father.

Churchill was a leader who influenced my life too. Before Churchill died, his friends suggested that any money raised after his death could go towards helping people to travel and learn from people in other countries. Churchill thought this was a great idea and after he died, his friends and family created a travelling fellowship for people who want to make a difference. I wanted to help young people dealing with grief and Churchill's fellowship helped me create a charity for bereaved children. I called it **Winston's Wish**. in his memory (www.winstonswish.org). The wish was that all bereaved children would get support to help them to grieve and rebuild their lives. Sometimes important things can happen after someone dies.

A lot of impressive leaders are often strengthened (rather than broken) by their experience of grief in their early years. They seem to find strength from it, even though they have experienced lonely and difficult times. Somehow their experience helps to shape them and encourage others to follow them.

Which leaders inspire you most? Maybe it is someone in your local community who helps others believe in themselves. A religious leader who helps people feel they belong. A sports coach who is helping others in their own time after work. The postman who looks out for and chats to people living alone as he delivers the post. All show great leadership. What qualities of leadership would you most like to show as you grow up and take your place in the world?

Battling with **grief** can sometimes even leave you feeling **stronger** and more **determined** than you were before you were bereaved.

CHAPTER 5

The coronavirus pandemic meant the whole world had to get used to wearing masks. I suspect you may have worn a mask yourself now and again too. Did you find the mask was a bit uncomfortable after a while, especially when it was hot? I also found it hard not being able to 'read' people's faces. I was unsure if they were happy or frustrated. Some people had very smiley eyes and that helped. What I do know is that it was often a big relief when we were able to remove our masks and relax.

The flexible feelings muscle

What has all this mask talk got to do with your grief? Well, when someone dies, people sometimes (often without meaning to) put on a kind of **invisible grief mask**. It is not a real mask, but it can mean that others are unsure about how you are really feeling. You may even forget how you are really feeling yourself. And the **flexible feelings muscle** knows that we have complete permission to let our feelings show and also at times to feel able to keep them private.

If it were a real mask it would probably have the words,

written on the front of it.

Let's see if you have tried one of these grief masks on yourself:

Do people sometimes say to you, 'how are you doing?'

Do you respond quickly, almost without thinking, with 'I'm FINE thanks!'

Does any of this sound familiar? Well, you are not alone …

Sue was a parent I knew who was finding life tough after her husband had died. Sue said that by **'fine'** she really meant that she was **F**ed up, **I**solated, **N**ervous and **E**xhausted!

Wearing a mask of grief can be a useful response when you really don't want to talk about it or if you want to avoid a conversation that could end up being awkward. If you say you're fine most people tend not to take the conversation further. We sometimes also say we're fine when deep down we are quite angry or sad but would prefer not to have to explain, in case it makes us lose control of our emotions when we are not comfortable to do so.

These invisible grief masks can help you to choose when you want to talk about things and equally when you don't – this is your **flexible feelings muscle** at work.

The **me** you
can't **see** . . .

Just because I am
smiling doesn't mean
I'm not **hurting**.

Danger alert!

Though a mask can be useful, it does become a problem if you keep your **grief mask** on most of the time. You can accidentally slip into a habit of never taking it off. You get used to saying 'I am fine' and **lock away** your feelings deep inside. Doing this can make the feelings more intense.

In trying to forget about those feelings, they can become bigger and more explosive. Bubbling away – they can start to become problematic. This is because keeping feelings locked deep underground can sometimes cause us to make bad choices. Instead of noticing how much something is hurting, you may find yourself wanting to lash out in anger or withdraw and go very quiet. Like a **simmering volcano** that eventually blows. So, you need to try and let them out now and again and talk about them with the people that you trust.

Angry volcano

Do you know that feeling, when you are upset, and you say you're fine, but people keep asking and asking and eventually you blow up like a big angry volcano? This is a normal reaction to frustration and grief, but it's important that the power of your anger doesn't hurt you or those around you. Sometimes just noticing what's simmering underneath and talking is a good start to relieving the pressure.

Can you see the smiling face at the top of the angry volcano on the previous page? Underneath, the pressure and heat is building ... have you noticed all those simmering angry thoughts that are bubbling away? The thoughts in the picture of the volcano belonged to a boy named Kordell after his brother Ty was stabbed by a gang.

What thoughts would you put in your volcano? Is anything simmering?

It's always best to avoid the erupting volcano, so start by trying to notice any angry thoughts that may be building up inside. Grab your notebook and draw your own **angry volcano**. Write down the things that are going through your head and maybe show them to a family member or a friend. Perhaps together you can think up some ways that could help you let off steam in a much gentler way than erupting. It could be dancing to very loud music, going for a run, learning martial arts or playing sports with your friends. Whatever it is, it will help give your mind a rest and get you feeling better again.

Stuck and silenced

I want to share Beth's story with you. We met each other when Beth was 13 and her mum had died nine months before. Beth's PE teacher Mrs Edgell had noticed that Beth had started to avoid games and was often away from school with a stomach bug or an ear infection. Beth found it impossibly hard to even mention her mum or how she had died. Beth had moved in with her dad and stepmum. This meant she now lived far away from her two best friends and had to share a bedroom with her eight-year-old stepsister. Even on top of her mum's death, SO many other things in Beth's life had changed. Everyone thought Beth was doing 'fine' except her teacher. The school discussed this with Beth's dad and they agreed that it could be useful for Beth to see someone like me. At first, Beth was unsure and wanted to be left alone. She knew her grades at school were very good and she said she was **fine**. It took a **lot** of effort from Mrs Edgell to persuade Beth to see me.

After we had built trust with each other, I showed Beth the memory stones. She held tightly to the rough rock and thought carefully before she eventually spoke. She whispered that she had an argument about cleaning her school shoes on the morning her mum died. She said that her mum left the house angry. On her way to work a lorry hit her mum's car and her mum had died instantly.

Beth had built up the small argument into a very big thing. She just couldn't express her grief. She was numb, she felt guilty and her confidence was at rock bottom. Beth also was waking up at night in a panic with horrible images of the crash (which she hadn't seen in reality).

I asked Beth, 'Do you think you caused your mum to die?'. She instantly looked up and quietly said 'yes'. I then asked, 'When you argued with your mum about cleaning your school shoes, did you intend that she might die?' Beth instantly said more forcefully 'NO, of course not!'

Of course, Beth wasn't to blame for her mum's death, but because her last encounter with her mum was this annoying argument, the idea had been eating her up inside. Beth was pretending she was **fine**, but she was hiding a story that she needed to share with someone she could trust. By **removing her mask**, Beth could allow herself to let go of the unhelpful guilt and traumatic crash pictures in her mind that were blocking her grief. At the end of our time together Beth decorated her memory box, which she then filled with good memories. Once she had finished, she shared it with her younger stepsister to explain how much she loved her mum. Sometimes when grief becomes so stuck, it takes a while to unblock it to make way for all the lovely pebble and gemstone memories (pages 85–9) that you might not feel ready to embrace yet. This kind of complicated grief is so important to untangle so you can let go of the festering feelings that drag you down and drain your energy. Are there parts of your grief that are more complicated – parts that you might need some more professional help to mend? You can ask an adult to call one of the helplines at the back of the book or look at the websites to see what may be local to you.

Trauma tips

I mentioned before that particularly horrible memories often won't go away. These very painful memories are sometimes called **traumatic memories**. They are also different as they often come into your mind uninvited. The vivid pictures that appear are sometimes called **flashbacks**. Traumatic memories can also happen in the night as nightmares. They are distressing, but talking about them and addressing what has happened can help you to feel more in control of the traumatic memory and slowly you can start to feel less afraid of it. Beth needed to do this.

Here are a few tips if you have any frightening images relating to the death that pop into your mind. The first step is to properly notice these images. This will allow you to deal with them and store them efficiently in your brain, so they take up less space.

Now notice any difficult thoughts. Draw these thoughts out as simple stick pictures and start to notice the feelings that go with them. Put a thick black line around each picture to frame it and contain it securely. **Note:** this work is best done with someone who can carefully support you as you explore these particularly painful feelings.

Fold up the pictures you have drawn as tiny as you can make them and throw them away. Imagine a wastepaper bin with loosely scrunched up papers. And another bin with the same amount of paper but carefully folded. The folded paper takes up much less space and most importantly leaves **space** for your **better memories.**

If you are still having scary memories, I have also included some good links to some helpful organisations at the back of the book. Please do ask an adult you trust to call them. They will be able to give help and advice just in case you need to go and see someone about these more complicated and traumatic memories. Traumatic memories can be so strong that they block your grief, so it's very important to not let this happen.

Courage, confidence and grit muscles

One person who needed a lot of courage, confidence and grit is **Jennifer Hudson**. An award-winning American actor who has a powerful singing voice, Jennifer was also a coach on *The Voice*.

In 2008 her life changed very suddenly when a policeman came to tell her that her mother, her brother and her seven-year-old nephew had been murdered. The man who murdered them had been a part of their family, as he had been married to Jennifer's sister.

It is possible that some of you reading this book may also be trying to make sense of a death in your family because of **murder** or **manslaughter**. You will already know that this is a very tough type of grief and your brain may be exhausted by vivid images of things that you saw or pictures that your brain is now imagining.
There are special groups of people who help with traumatic deaths

and the helplines at the back will be able to suggest how you can meet others. You can also ask your police family liaison officer for some helpful contacts.

Jennifer took a year away from performing to allow herself to grieve quietly at home and to cope with the more public trial that she attended each day with her sister. After that year she found the strength to sing the National Anthem to start the Super Bowl. Jennifer's son David was born a year later. Jennifer talks about David inspiring her to rebuild her life and look to the future. Her mother had a strong faith in God and encouraged her children to always talk if they were hurting and try to see the **positives** in life. Jennifer remembered her mother's words and wrote a song to help her on difficult days, and she sings, 'my momma taught me everything I know, and I will take it everywhere I go ...'

I want you to be like Jennifer – able to find your **voice, help others** and **also ask for help** when you need it.

The elephant in the room

Being silent with grief can happen in families or friendship groups too. Though it's better to be able to have those courageous conversations with each other - it can sometimes feel quite awkward. How is your family or friendship circle finding it? Can you all talk openly and easily about the person who has died? If so, I am very pleased because many people find this hard to do.

Sharing your memories, possibly using your memory box or your stones, is often a good way to start. But this is not always straightforward – a boy I know called Sanjay told me he was worried he would upset his dad with his grief, so he learnt to 'button it up' after his Nani had died from cancer.

When no one talks about something that is big and important, we sometimes describe this as having an 'elephant in the room' – it's like sitting having your dinner together with a **huge** elephant on the table and pretending it isn't there. It may be that everyone cares deeply but **no one talks about it**. It's like it hasn't happened. Everyone is busy and getting on with life and no one really knows how each other really feels. But people are all so very different. For families or friends feeling alone with this awkward elephant it is not so easy.

Grief is a very **individual** experience. How do you think others are coping? People around you may want to express their grief in different ways. It's important to talk and work out ways that allow people to remember someone in ways they feel are right for them.

I remember not being that keen to return to Cornwall each year to lay flowers on my dad's grave on his birthday. My mum and brother loved to make the journey. At first, I think my mum felt very disappointed and quite angry with me for not going on this annual visit to my dad's grave. Eventually I was brave enough to explain that this trip did not work for me and I liked to think about dad in my own ways. On this occasion my mum listened. Dad and I used to enjoy keeping tropical fish and he also loved music. So, my way of thinking about him was to arrange for an old upright piano to be upcycled into a fish tank. Every day when I feed my fish in my piano aquarium, I feel I am saying **hello to my dad**.

It might be time for your family or friends to have a **courageous conversation** about what works best for different people and discuss anything that you do want to do together to remember the person who has died. Your **flexible feelings muscle** is so helpful as it enables you to show your feelings or not show your feelings – to share them or not share them when you want to be more private.

One family I met really impressed me as they worked hard to figure out how to share their grief. The father of Steph (17), Sarah (14) and Jack (eight) had died suddenly on Boxing Day. The family were completely devastated. They were all at different stages in their lives and that affected how they grieved. For a while, an **elephant was in the room**. It was harder to talk. Steph was doing her exams and had a boyfriend who supported her. Jack was younger and was brilliant at sport. The whole family loved their dad so much, but it seemed to Sarah that others in the family found it a little easier to let go and get on with their lives.

Eventually the family began to share their experiences of grief. After a year or so they spoke more about their feelings and wanted to create something that united them. They decided to organise a wonderful **Boxing Day Challenge** to raise funds for a charity that had helped them after their dad died. Every year on Boxing Day hundreds of people would turn up to walk or run and remember someone who had died. Not only was it a great thing to do to raise money, but it also meant that families knew there was a time over the Christmas break when they could walk or run in memory of someone. The family united around a common purpose of remembering their lovely dad on the anniversary of the day he died.

There are many ways you can work together to find ways to grieve that not only suit you individually, but also as a group. Now let's think again about your family or group of friends. Do you have any little or even big elephants in the room that need discussing? Do you feel brave enough to use your **flexible feelings muscle** and have one of those courageous conversations? There is one particular question that we will tackle now that can be tricky for some families to talk about.

What if another **person** dies? What will happen to <u>**me**</u>?

Really BIG questions for families

There is one particular concern that comes up a lot when I speak to young people who have lost a family member. **What if somebody else dies?** They often want to know what would happen to them if someone else in their family dies – and especially the person who looks after them. This may not be relevant to some of you reading this book, but for those who may be worried about what would happen to them, I promise to be honest. I will give you an exercise that allows you to face up to your fears.

My nan knew me very well, so if I went very quiet, she could tell I was probably worrying about something. She would gently remind me that,

If something is **mentionable**, it's **manageable**.

She was right. Talking about something you are worried about **will not** make it more likely to happen. It will, however, make it more likely that you can put it to one side and concentrate on your life in the here and now.

If you say, 'But what happens if you die too?' adults will often want to say, 'Oh you don't need to worry about that! I am never ever going to leave you', and then try and change the subject, as this is a fear they worry about too. Though it's comforting to hear them say they will never leave you, young people tell me that pushing this fear under the carpet doesn't make it go away. **They do want to know the disaster plan even if that plan is never needed.**

The example on the next few pages is a situation where Rory had two parents at home, and then one parent died. Rory was 12 and he now lived with his mum and younger sister. His dad had died very suddenly at home six months before. I know Rory's family set-up may not be the same as yours, so you may need to adapt this exercise to your own personal situation. It may be useful to show the Tall Wall of Worries example on the following pages to the adult or adults who care for you so they can help you understand the plans that are in place in the very **unlikely** event that they will die too when you are still a child.

THE TALL WALL of WORRIES

To give you an idea of how it helps to look at fears calmly and logically, let's go back in time to a wise philosopher from ancient Greece called Socrates.

Socrates was awesome at asking questions that helped his students to think through exceptionally **tough** situations. He noticed that occasionally emotions can get in the way, so he wanted to help his students with logical thinking. He trained his students by asking the **same question** several times, allowing them time to reflect and answer in between each question.

I call this exercise the **Tall Wall of Worries**. We can use this Socratic questioning technique to get down from the wall safely.

Let's imagine Rory asks the big question, **'what happens if my mum dies too?'** Imagine he's standing at the very top of a very high wall. At first it's so scary and overwhelming that Rory can barely get the question out.

Socrates guides him down a few steps by asking,

'IF THAT WERE TO HAPPEN, WHAT IS IT THAT WORRIES YOU?'

Being able to talk this fear through was important and a great relief to Rory.

Rory steps down a further level and replies,

'My mum has told me she has made a will which means our auntie will look after us. She is our guardian and she lives in Scotland.'

'IF THAT WERE TO HAPPEN, WHAT IS IT THAT WORRIES YOU?'

Rory thinks about it, takes a deep breath, steps onto a much lower part of the wall and says,

'Depending on our age, my sister and I would probably have to move to Scotland. We would have to make new friends.'

'IF THAT WERE TO HAPPEN, WHAT IS IT THAT WORRIES YOU?'

Rory notices his body feels a little calmer and takes another several steps down and replies,

'We may not have our own bedrooms and I would worry that we may not make new friends quickly.'

'RORY, THINK ABOUT THIS NEXT QUESTION VERY CAREFULLY. USE ALL YOUR GRIEF MUSCLES. IF THAT WERE TO HAPPEN, WHAT WOULD BE SO BAD ABOUT THAT? AND WHAT WOULD SOMEONE YOU TRULY ADMIRE SAY TO YOU?'

As instructed, Rory thought about it very carefully. He chose to think about what his dad might say.

'I guess if my sister and I can stay together that's most important. I think my dad would say to me you're great at sport Rory — join the hockey team straight away and that way you will make friends quickly.'

Rory was now on firmer ground. He (and his mum) had faced right into his worst fear and carried it down to a manageable level. Sometimes these biggest fears and worries do need to be noticed and discussed. Rory spoke to his mum, discovered there was a back-up plan for the very unlikely chance something would happen to her. His fear was now manageable. It had been mentioned.

You can do this too. Whatever it is that you are worrying about, imagine speaking with Socrates and slowly climbing down the worry wall by repeating and answering the same questions. Just like Rory, you will be able to come up with a **solution** for the situation that is worrying you and feel much more reassured.

It is worth saying that these big worries will most often never actually happen, but sometimes we need to talk through the fear to be freed up and get on with life.

Giving back happiness

After someone has died, people often like to do something meaningful to help others. Have you heard of a band called **One Direction**? They are one of the bestselling boy bands of all time. One of the members of the band, **Louis Tomlinson**, experienced grief when his mum Johanna died from leukaemia at the age of 43. She was an important influence in Louis' life and shortly after she died, he released the song *Just Hold On.*

A family tragedy then struck again, two years later, when Louis' 19-old-sister Felicity died.

This was an incredibly hard few years of intense grief. However, he reflects on how it helps him manage smaller everyday hassles when something so big has happened.

'Maybe because I've had real dark moments in my life, they've given me scope for optimism. In the grand scheme of things, of what I've experienced, these everyday problems ... they don't seem so bad.'

Do you ever think this way – because you've experienced something that is **big**, it somehow helps you not to worry so much about the smaller stuff?

Louis has over 35 million followers on Twitter and he frequently checks in with fans who are grieving. He has also done lots of charity work and quietly supports children and young people who are seriously ill and may die. He likes to do this privately and without any fuss. He's also developed a **grief mindset** to help him bounce back from difficult days. Occasionally when you're famous some of those difficult days are when people write hurtful and untrue things about you. On a bad press or social media day, he said he speaks directly to his mum in his head and says to himself, 'Come on mum, let's make someone happy today.' Clearly Louis believes in focussing on helping others rather than focussing on things with negative energy. He will then seek out someone who is having a tough time that he can try to make happy. What a great way to choose to turn a difficult day into a special day for someone else.

Can you think of some things that you can do to make someone happy today?

We have covered a lot of ground and you've worked hard on all your grief activities. It's now time to take a rest and discover the importance of resting and playing when you are grieving. **Play** is usually fun, it's relaxing and it creates **energy**. It helps you to use your imagination and can distract your brain from all the tough feelings you are dealing with. Your brain is working in overdrive, so it does need plenty of time to rest and refuel.

The balance muscle

In this chapter we're going to look at flexing your **balance** muscle. This muscle is useful to keep a check on four areas that really help you balance the demands of grief.

SLEEPING, EATING, MOVING and CREATING

SLEEPING: getting a good night's sleep when you are grieving is important to properly rest both your mind and your body.

Sleep will really help you restore your energy when you are grieving.

Ideally you want to be getting around eight to ten hours of good sleep every night. How do you do this? Well, you probably know some of the tricks already – take a warm bath or shower (not hot) before bed. Keep the lights dim and turn screens off. Read quietly or listen to a good story or gentle music. Doing some gentle deep breathing exercises to help calm your body and mind before you drift off to sleep can really help you **relax**. But if your brain is still feeling really busy with lots of thoughts whooshing around, you can sleep with a notebook by your bed so that if you do wake up in the middle of the night, you can scribble down your thoughts and go back to sleep settled.

Sleep is a time when your body and mind can rest and repair after being so busy in the daytime. While we sleep and dream our brains are unconsciously still at work sorting things out. I found that when I was writing this book I would wake up early after a good night's sleep with an idea that seemed to fit well. And I would feel pleased that somehow my brain was still looking after me as I slept.

However, if occasionally you have a really bad night's sleep, you might find you wake up feeling drained and you need what is sometimes called a **'duvet day'**. You know those days when you can't face having to deal with people? You just want to rest and snuggle down under the duvet, feel safe, snooze and dream. It's important not to get into a habit of avoiding things because of grief, but some duvet days in the first year may help when everything is just too much.

Sleeping without worry

Let me tell you about Amy. She had a little bag of **worry dolls** that she made out of pegs. (You can also buy them if you don't want to make them yourself.) The idea comes from Guatemala. According to legend, Guatemalan children tell one worry to each doll before they go to bed and place the dolls under their pillow. In the morning the dolls have made the worries feel a lot smaller and manageable. Amy used her worry dolls after her best friend died. It was so shocking to Amy that someone her age could die and was never coming back. It set off all sorts of other worries, but telling a worry to each of the dolls every night helped Amy to cope and not feel quite so overwhelmed.

If you're not a doll-type person, you may prefer to hang a **dream catcher** over your bed. Some people say that good dreams drift down through the feathers and beads hanging down off the dream catcher, whilst difficult or scary dreams get trapped in the web.

EATING: your body needs fuel so you can recharge. It also helps with a lack of energy.

The trouble is that people can find that eating is not so straightforward after someone dies. Some people go completely off their food for a while. It's like their digestive system shuts down with the shock. Other people say that after a while they notice they are eating more – especially sugary treats and fast food. This is called comfort eating. If you have any worries about the best way to ensure you get **good nutrition**, do ask someone to help you eat well. Eating nutritious foods will help with your mood and improve your energy levels.

Food is often very comforting and can be linked to our emotions. Are there special foods that remind you of the person you are remembering or are there any recipes you want to put in your **memory box** that they liked to make? Are there any dates when it would be good to use the recipe to remind you of the person who has died?

INTERESTING FACT:
Did you know that lots of celebrity chefs were bereaved as children? People such as Nigel Slater, Marco Pierre White, Rick Stein, Lisa Faulkner and many others. They have said that their love of cooking delicious food helped them to feel connected to the important people in their lives who had died.

MOVING: this is so important for increasing your energy, clearing your mind and helping you to feel less stressed. Moving around can also be lots of fun!

Being active is great for developing the **grit muscle**. Lots of very successful sports heroes have said they used sport to help them focus after someone had died. They set their sights on dreaming about a particular goal and it gave them something to focus on.

Is there a sport that you love? Or maybe there is a new activity you can try? How can you sweat out some of your sadness? Simply moving around helps – walking in nature or dancing to music can also be a great way to improve your mood and energy levels.

As well as moving, learning how to do breathing exercises will help calm you down and rest your body. **Square breathing** is a very calming exercise. Imagine a square and then imagine slowly tracing your finger from the top-left corner across to the right-hand corner, breathing in as you do so. Follow the line down to the bottom-right corner and slowly breathe out. Continue around the square, taking nice slow breaths in and calming, slow breaths out.

Tom Daley is an Olympic medal-winning diver. He represented Great Britain at the 2008 Summer Olympics when he was just 14 – the youngest person from any nation to participate in a diving final that year. At the time, Tom's dad was having treatment for a brain tumour. His dad sadly died in 2011, just a few days after Tom's 17th birthday. A year later in 2012, Tom won a bronze medal at the London Olympics. Tom is a big fan of using breathing to help him relax and feel less anxious. He once said, '... just taking ten seconds to focus on my breathing in the morning, at night or even when I am on the [diving] board about to compete, really helps me forget any worries about what might have happened or could happen and just live in the present.'

CREATING: getting creative can help you to relax and also improve your mood.

Doing what you love is so important for you right now. Maybe you like to **paint** or draw? Or **grow** things? Perhaps you like to **make** things, write poems or make music and write songs? You might like playing computer games or coding.

It doesn't matter what, so long as it allows you to be creative and to get energy from creating something you **love**. Music can be especially helpful with grief. It can allow feelings to surface and it can encourage you to simply go on and never give up. Lots of young people find it helpful to write music and songs after experiencing such a big loss.

Grieving can be **exhausting**, so as well as eating, sleeping and getting some movement into your day, don't forget to **be kind to yourself**.

Music can help to heal your hurt

Two of the most famous singer-songwriters in the world both met shortly after their mothers died. **Paul McCartney** and **John Lennon**. They were in a band called The Beatles. Have you heard of them?

The song *Let It Be* was very important to Paul. He wrote it thinking about his mum, Mary. It's a great example of writing a song to help you through tough times. The song helps Paul to feel that his mother is always with him.

Let it be is a little phrase that is often used to encourage people who are angry or fighting something or someone - to simply let it go, relax, try not to worry about your troubles. 'Let it be' were the words his mum would say when she would need to stop Paul and his brothers and sisters squabbling – you know the way that brothers and sisters do. He says that he wrote the song as it gave him a sense of comfort to know she was close by, especially in times of trouble when he wanted her wise words to guide him.

It's a lovely song, comforting, hopeful and positive. It gave Paul the reassurance to imagine his mum will **always be with him** when he needs her most.

Do you like writing songs or poetry? Could you maybe compose something and keep it in your memory box?

To help you to get started with your creative thoughts maybe you could think about how you would answer the statements below and then turn it into a poem or song:

If they could come back just for five minutes this is what I would want them to know . . .

Things they did or said that guide me now . . .

What they would be proud of in terms of how I have coped . . .

'**A**s each year goes by my grief has grown up with me, some days it still hurts more than others. That's okay and I'm okay.'

Zara was three when her dad died. On the 20th anniversary after his death, she wrote this note.

'From what I hear my dad was a pretty cool guy ... but that's not what I miss about him. I miss him not being here for my 11th, 12th and 18th birthday, not being there at my graduation, not being there to ask a second opinion and, most importantly, not being there to know what being there would've been like ... I am lucky though, as I had a lot of people who were there ... my mum's an absolute legend. She's strong. I'm lucky.'

As Zara was reflecting on the 20 years without her dad, she giggled as she remembered a picture she drew for her **memory box.**

'Aged six I drew the most spectacular family portrait: Mum, my brother and I, dad on a cloud and this lovely gentleman stood next to my mum.
"And who's that?" mum asked.
"Oh that's David Beckham," I replied.

'It's fair to say I had great taste at a very young age!'

Time passes gently and slowly on the grief path. It was Zara who felt like she had an **apple** stuck in her throat – when it was so difficult to find the right words, ones that wouldn't cause people to struggle to know what to say back. Now Zara can talk openly about her grief.

This chapter is about looking forward to your **future**. To see where you have come from and to think about the future path you may take as you carry your grief with you into adulthood, using some good **grief muscles** you have developed over time, and this toolkit that you've picked up along the way.

Getting over it?

It's odd how people sometimes ask if you are **'over it'** in a matter of weeks or months. Maybe they are just hoping that you are feeling happier, yet it can feel like a very confusing question. Especially if the person who died was a very **big** part of your life.

Strangely, even though grief can be very draining (especially at first), people often say that it's something they want to keep. They want to be able to hold on to the emotions but not be overwhelmed by them. In the drawings that follow, the first three circles show how other people may **assume** grief fits into your world.

This represents you at the start of your grief, at the point when your person has just died. It can feel like a stormy ocean that you are trying to navigate in a small boat, and it **fills up your world**. Having so many strong emotions all at the same time takes so much energy, you may feel you have no energy for anything else in your life.

The second small circle (let's say six weeks later) is how others may **assume** things may start to feel as time moves on. The stormy ocean may have calmed a little, you are slowly getting better... aren't you?

Then after six months some people may begin to ask **'are you getting over it?'** You are no longer in that boat on the stormy ocean – the ocean is in fact just a few drops of water. So, people assume you must be almost **over it.** This is how grief works, right? **Wrong. It just doesn't work that way.**

The <u>reality</u> is that gradually ...

We learn to grow around our grief

MEMORIES

THEN NOW & ALWAYS

Grief Globe

The circle of grief may not be any smaller, but your **world** has
expanded to allow you **space** to rebuild. Grief gets easier to
manage – there's a lifebelt and a lighthouse to help guide you
away from the rocks when you are having a difficult day.
Growing around your grief gives you room for taking chances,
trying new things, even a bit of belly laughing! Some days these

intensely sad feelings certainly return, a bit like mine did briefly on the day I went to see the Queen, but you won't be so overwhelmed by them. It is as if those **grief muscles** have helped you expand your world, made it bigger and stronger. There is more space. More oxygen to breathe and now you can move forward. Some days you might find yourself again on that boat, and the ocean may be a little rough, but your grief and your memories are all safe inside – just no longer so overwhelming.

Some people also tell me that although they would **never** have wanted the person to die, grief has opened up a new way of thinking about everything. They are somehow now even more grateful for things that they previously took for granted. Having a sense of **gratitude** improves your grit. It helps you to appreciate life and the people in it. Because you really know what it is like to lose someone, you choose to live life to its fullest.

Saying hello, not goodbye

Do you recall right back in the introduction I mentioned the need sometimes to be able to talk openly and honestly with people? Well, we also need to be able to speak **openly** and **honestly** with the person who has died. Clearly those conversations will now be held in our hearts and minds as the person is no longer here to speak with directly. This section is all about continuing conversations with the person who has died so you can find a sense of peace with what's happened and can face the future with hope.

So now it is time to create something very special to put into your memory box. It is time to have a very **important conversation** directly with them just in case there is anything that feels unfinished, anything that you would like them to know but didn't have the chance to tell them when they were alive.

I hope it will help you to have that conversation by giving you the beginning of a sentence and then asking you to finish it off. This is one of those exercises that you may want to do with someone who is a good listener. They may also ask you a few follow-up questions after you answer just to make sure they understand how you are feeling. You may find it hard to think of an answer right away. If so, be kind to yourself, allow a bit of time and just see what comes up. And if you feel angry or disappointed about some things that's okay – try to be as honest as you can. You are about to create a ...

Little Box of Big Thoughts.

First, find a box (something small, the size of a pack of playing cards, a soap box or a nice envelope will work well). Next, make 20 small cards that fit into it. On each card write the beginning of a sentence that you will then finish either in writing or on your phone or computer. (I have given you the sentences on the next two pages.) You may find that some of these questions might be harder to answer, so just take your time, answer them in the order I have written them and see what bubbles up from deep down inside. Some answers may be funny or loving. However, I do also know that nobody is perfect. Even people who die are not perfect. So, it may be that in some of your answers you also allow yourself to say those things too. If that is the case, well done, this is all about being **honest** and **brave** - not just with the easy memories but including any more difficult bits of your story.

INSTRUCTIONS

1. Start each card with Dear.................... (name of the person).
2. Next, write the first 'conversation starter' below on your card, and fill in the rest with your person in mind.
3. Sign and date the card and then if you like, start on the next one.
4. Fold up your cards and store them in your little box or envelope and keep them safe in your memory box.

* I hope that you . . .

* Always know that . . .

* I feel so proud when . . .

* I laugh when . . .

* I wish . . .

* I remember when . . .

* I regret . . .

* It was your choice to . . .

* Thank you for . . .

* You would shine when . . .

* When times get tough . . .

* I love you because . . .

* Now we're not together, what I miss most about you is . . .

* You are special because . . .

* ❋ I hope that I can be more . . .
* ❋ I will try to be less . . .
* ❋ Sometimes I feel we are similar because . . .
* ❋ Something that really matters in my family life . . .
* ❋ A favourite memory I will always have is . . .
* ❋ Then, now and always . . .

If you have access to a computer and a printer and would prefer to print out the cards, you can download a PDF at:
https://geni.us/LittleBoxOfBigThoughts

After you have done this, think about how you felt having that conversation with the person who has died. Did some answers make you laugh? Maybe some brought tears of relief to have finally said it out loud? You may find that emotions particularly come up if you share them with someone. It's a **big** exercise. That's why I call it a Little Box of **big** Thoughts. Keep your answers safe in your memory box. It will be interesting to re-read them as you get older. You may even want to see how differently you might answer the same questions over the next year or two.

I'd like you to meet Tom. Tom was younger when his dad died, but after his 12th birthday he decided to complete a **Little Box of Big Thoughts** each year on his dad's birthday. He finds it a good way of staying connected as he grows and develops. For his mum's birthday he made a set of cards that he filled in with his thoughts on her, as he knew she was struggling with her grief and missing his dad. She loved to read how her son felt and sleeps with them under her pillow as she finds them such a **comfort**. Is there someone else in your life who you might like to give a Little Box of Big Thoughts to?

Your strengths

We have talked a lot about staying strong, but interestingly, one thing I haven't asked you yet is about your own particular strengths. Let's do this! It's fun to think about the specific strengths that you have and how they will help you in life. To make it easier I have put lots of different strengths on the next page for you to consider.

Can you select what you think are your **top ten** strengths from the suggestions shown? Please add some of your own if they are not on there. If you are up for it, I would encourage you to ask someone else's opinion about your strengths. Ask them what they think are your top ten strengths. It would be great if you can ask about three or four different people and see which ones (if any) are the same. You will know if one is a particularly strong strength if it is noticed by several other people. The **confidence muscle** loves **feedback**. Not always because what they say is true, but because it's a gift to realise how others see you.

To get you started, here is selection of some of the **strengths** you might have.

I am sensible

I am strong

I am good at making things

I think a lot

I am a calm person

I am good fun

I am good at sport

I am loving

I help other people

I am an interesting person

I will try new things

I see things through to the end

I can be trusted

I am fair

I can change

I have good manners

I am neat and tidy

I am careful

I am happy

I tell people what I think

I am brave

I don't waste anything

I am easy to get along with

I do things with others

I make people laugh/smile

I am a good friend

I work hard

I am honest

I can do things by myself

I care about other people's feelings

I am patient

I bounce back when I am hurt

I can do things well and quickly

I am kind

I stick up for myself

I am good at doing things

I am full of energy

I forgive people when they make mistakes

I can find a way to do things

I am good at looking after things

Now we have a note of your top ten strengths, it's time to create your **Tree of Life**. I really am excited for you to do this exercise. You have worked so hard to get to this point and the Tree of Life will help to remind you of how you are coping with grief as a young person. It will be great to keep in your memory box too.

First, take a look at our **example tree** on pages 194–5. Next, grab yourself some pens and a **large** piece of plain paper and draw a big tree in the centre, with a wide trunk, long branches that stretch out and deep long roots that will keep your tree firm in the ground.

STEP ONE
THE TRUNK – strengths

This is a strong tree. It will not get blown over in the wind or a gale or even a hurricane. The trunk on a tree gets stronger as the tree gets older. The trunk is the part of the tree that connects the leafy crown to its roots. The trunk is the messenger of growth from the roots to the leaves.

Now, on the **TRUNK** there's space for you to write your top ten strengths. Write them in your trunk or next to it if there's not enough space.

STEP TWO

THE ROOTS - your values

The roots of a tree are very important. The roots suck water and nutrients out of the soil to feed the tree. The roots are not only good for the tree, they are also good for the soil. When it rains the roots hold the soil in place, so it is not washed away.

Finding your roots will help you to be clear about your values. The words you write on your roots should be the things that are important to you - your **values**. Some of these values are passed on from previous generations, including the values you may want to hold on to from people who are no longer alive. You will feel most satisfied when you are able to see your values in the way you live your life now and in the future.

You can see from the example on pages 194-5 that the values are about being honest, courageous, never giving up, adding value to the world by caring for others and showing respect and gratitude. What are some of the values that are important to you and maybe also your family or friendship group? What values keep you on the right path when you make choices about how to live your life? What do you believe is super important?

STEP THREE
THE BRANCHES - your dreams

And then we have these wonderful branches that stretch up and out towards the sun. The branches represent your **hopes** and **dreams** for the future. Maybe it's something you want to become good at, a job you think you would enjoy doing, your dreams and hopes for your family or friends ... maybe you want a pet? Perhaps you want to go somewhere special in the world? Or maybe you want to be happy and content? Just sit back and think to yourself – what do I want the branches in my tree of life to reach out towards? Write down three big dreams that you would just love to happen in the future and three smaller things that you would also like to see happen sooner. If you have more, write these down too.

STEP FOUR
THE LEAVES - your key people

Now we need to add some evergreen leaves to your tree.
Your leaves represent:

* ✳ people in your life now who you **trust**

* ✳ people who you **respect**

* ✳ people who **encourage you**

* ✳ people who make you **smile**

* ✳ all your **friends and family** who are important to you

✳ maybe there are one or two famous people you might want to add who **inspire you**

Write their names on separate leaves. You may have just a few leaves or if you have a larger family or group of friends you may have a lot – choose the people who matter most. You can also include people such as a teacher who understands you or a coach who is helping you to become good at something.

STEP FIVE
THE SUN – your energy

Finally, we need a sun so that the tree can grow strong and healthy. On the rays of your sun write down **five things** that give you **energy** now. The things that are helping you to have the energy to cope with your grief. The energisers that spark joy and help you to feel happier and hopeful.

There, you have done it – you have drawn your very own strong and hopeful **Tree of Life**. Stand back, look at it and allow yourself to feel proud. No one else will have the same tree because you are **unique**. And if challenging things happen to you in the future, anything that feels tough – get this tree out from your memory box to remind yourself of what makes you strong and hopeful. Your tree will change as your life changes and yet some bits of this tree may never change. Be sure to put the date on your tree and how old you were at the time. Maybe do another tree in five years' time and notice any changes.

My Tree of Life

Gives me Energy

- Chatting with my friends
- Playing video games with my brother
- Going for a run
- Bike rides with Jake
- Movie night with mum

DREAMS

- Aunt Laura
- To become a vet
- My teacher
- To get a dog of my own
- Jake

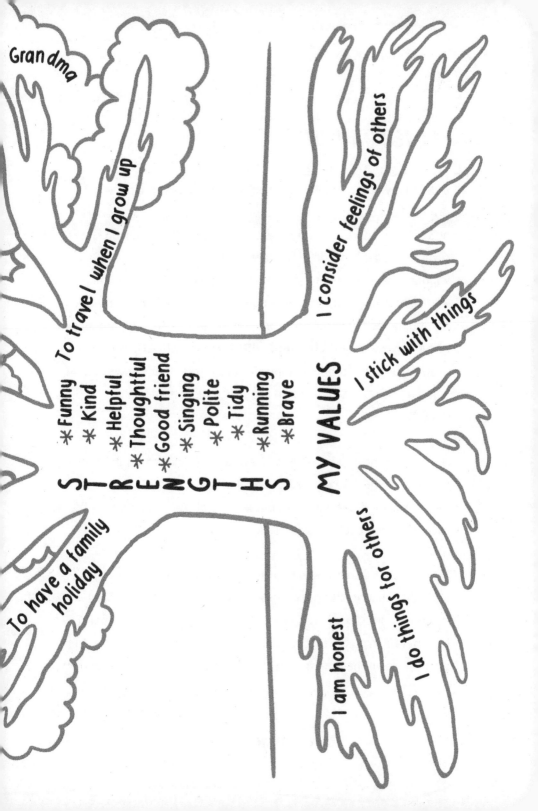

Grandma

To travel when I grow up

I consider feelings of others

I stick with things

STRENGTHS

*Funny
*Kind
*Helpful
*Thoughtful
*Good friend
*Singing
*Polite
*Tidy
*Running
*Brave

MY VALUES

To have a family holiday

I am honest

I do things for others

I LOVE YOU MUM

In 2012 it was a very big year in London. It was the year of the London Olympics and everyone across the UK was feeling very proud of our athletes. We expected to get medals in some sports and in other sports we were less confident. We had not won an Olympic medal for Judo in 12 years. This story is about a young woman who beat the French world champion Audrey Tcheuméo to win a silver medal. It's also a story that showed the world how grief tapped her on the shoulder in one of the most important moments in her life. Her name is **Gemma Gibbons**. And when Gemma was growing up and attending competitions, her mother's encouraging voice would regularly be heard shouting out from the gallery **'Come on, Gem!'**

Before Gemma was born her dad left, so her mum brought Gemma up herself. She worked hard and as Gemma once explained in an interview, 'we didn't have a lot of money and she dedicated her life to helping me reach my potential.'

In 2004 when Gemma was 17, her mum was diagnosed with a type of blood cancer called leukaemia. Although this can be treated, the treatment didn't work for Gemma's mum and tragically, six months later her mum died. The Olympics took place eight years later, 20 minutes down the road from where Gemma had lived with her mum.

Gemma's grandmother said: *'I think her mum's death made Gemma even more determined to succeed.'*

Millions of viewers around the world were watching Gemma in a very tough match against the world champion. At the moment when it was clear that she had won, Gemma sunk to her knees weeping and spontaneously looked up and mouthed the words

'I LOVE YOU, MUM'

The silent tears and silent words that Gemma mouthed were noticed by millions of people. In that moment we all witnessed how grief became her **friend**. It naturally allowed Gemma to share her brilliant achievement with the person who mattered most – her mum. The sports commentators wept and even the Prime Minister at the time, David Cameron, personally spoke to Gemma on her achievement. It was not just her sporting achievement that he noticed. Just like you, he could also see how she had worked hard to develop all those **grief muscles** to find a way through. Grief can unite people. David Cameron's young son Ivan had died three years before.

When a journalist asked Gemma about her spontaneous message to her mum she simply said, 'I didn't get to thank my mum, so that was a kind of thanks to her. I felt I would have definitely **made her proud** today. She was everything to me.'

Happy tears...
Even though they
may not be here
to witness your
happiness,
they can be in
your **heart** –

THEN · NOW & · ALWAYS

Have you watched the Disney film *The Lion King*? In the film, the young cub Simba is forced to leave the Pride Lands after his father Mufasa is murdered by his wicked uncle, Scar. Years later, he returns as a strong young lion ready to reclaim his throne and lead his tribe.

But first Simba goes off on his own **grief adventure**. For quite a while he feels very alone and lost. He has great fun with Timon the meerkat and Pumbaa the warthog – his funny friends who cheered him up and helped distract him from his grief. Eventually he allows his special trust buddies Nala and Zazu to get close and guide him. At times he is even confident enough to show his anger and tears with them. Simba sadly felt terrible guilt as he thought he had contributed to his father's death in a stampede. He hadn't, but that guilt took him on a very complicated and lonely path. He was in the **F**ed Up , **I**solated , **N**ervous and **E**xhausted version of **FINE**. But in the film, you see how Simba starts to build his grief muscles and begins to believe in himself again. There is a great song in the film called *Circle of Life*, which is played at the beginning when Simba is born, and again at the end when he returns to his homeland the leader of the tribe.

There are gazillions of **grief paths**. Simba took his path, and you will take yours. There will be junctions where you will make choices on how you use those grief muscles to think about things as they crop up.

Grief muscles

Let's remind ourselves of all seven grief muscles and how they can help you now and in the future:

1. TRUST – Choosing to talk openly with people who understand and listen

2. CONFIDENCE – Being sure of yourself

3. MEMORY – Building a memory store that can comfort and reassure you

4. GRIEF MINDSET – Beliefs that help you grow beyond your loss

5. GRIT – Finding your inner strength and looking forward

6. FLEXIBLE FEELINGS – Showing them, not showing them. Sharing them, not sharing them

7. BALANCE – Finding time to rest and play. Holding on to the past, and letting go to rebuild your life

When a death happens, it casts a shadow on your childhood. It takes quite a while for the sun to shine again. The illustration on the front cover of this book represents how turbulent grief can be. You need strength to keep the boat on course and to notice the people who are shining a light to help guide you safely to shore and throwing a lifebelt to support you.

LESSONS FROM LIAM

One young person who went through a very tough time as I was writing this book is a boy called **Liam**. He had just moved to big school when his family life changed dramatically. Three years before, family life had already changed a lot for Liam when his dad had left. Liam, now 12, told me that his grandad (who he saw every day) had died from the coronavirus. He struggled terribly at first as he wanted to see him in hospital before he died and could not visit. He knew these were the rules, but he was still **furious**. Liam was also secretly worried when he heard stories describing young people as 'super spreaders'. He worried about how his grandad had caught the virus, and on a bad day even worried that he may have given it to him. However, he never said a word to anyone. **He kept his grief firmly under wraps**. His volcano was in danger of erupting. It was like the anger he had felt three years earlier when his dad had left.

Liam's mum was in total shock at her dad's death. She felt she had lost everything and found it hard to notice how Liam was doing especially when he said he was fine. Liam wasn't really fine. He was also the fed up, isolated, nervous, and exhausted version of **fine**. He was furious too.

Liam was dragging around some heavy, **dark** feelings. He was getting into fights most days at school. He felt like exploding when anyone mentioned the virus, or when he saw it on the news. Liam could not speak about his grandad's death. It was too raw.

Anger was choking all his other feelings.

Liam was in the school cross-country squad. He had a brilliant year tutor, Mr Hopton, who knew him well (as he was regularly sent for detention by other teachers!). Mr Hopton could see beyond Liam's difficult behaviour and guessed that behind his **rage** he was hurting. Mr Hopton was no pushover – he was firm and friendly. Liam knew he could trust him.

One afternoon after school they found a safe, quiet space to create a **Little Box of Big Thoughts**. He did one for his grandad and another one for his dad (who was still alive but now lived abroad). They agreed that only Liam and Mr Hopton would read these cards. This allowed Liam to have a courageous conversation and to safely explore his anger, especially towards his dad. The anger gradually subsided and it gave way to terrible sadness. But it was a big relief. He felt he could begin to say goodbye to his grandad in his own way.

A few of the questions in the **Little Box of Big Thoughts** were hard to admit to – he could feel tears prickle in his eyes when he thought about his dad and grandad and all the things they used to do together. That was all gone now. But, Liam did stop waking up at night having the same nightmare about not being able to get into the hospital, and another nightmare about his dad leaving became less frequent. Mr Hopton also helped Liam to make a **memory box** with photos of his grandad.

Liam told me that he now goes around the house 'singing loud so they can hear.' He explained that his grandad loved Bruce Springsteen, so he plays a song by Bruce Springsteen – *Born to Run* – loud in his bedroom. When he was selected for the cross-country county team, he wrote his grandad a note and put it into his memory box. He is certainly **not over it**, but Liam is slowly getting **more used to it**. Liam and his mum are finding ways to slowly move forward. Some days are heavy going and some days feel calmer.

When I think about Liam's teacher noticing and helping him when he was struggling it makes me smile. I am also so proud when I think about Liam's courage to face up to his fears and anger. He even allowed Mr Hopton to witness his sadness a little bit. He used parts of his grief toolkit and is now growing up with grief in a healthy way. He looked for alternative ways to sweat out his feelings. His way. Long-distance running was also so important for Liam to manage his anger.

And just like you, Liam is beginning to train himself to use all of those **grief muscles**.

Tomorrow will be a good day

I hope that you will share some of what you have read with the people in your life who will support and help you to make good choices about how you go forward. These adults may be in your family or they may be a sports coach, a faith leader or perhaps a teacher you really like at school. You may also find there are people out there who have also been through this as a child and simply get it. Many of them have helped me in writing this book. One other person who inspired me was **Captain Sir Tom Moore**. You may have heard about him. He was 100 years old and during the pandemic he started to walk with his frame, one step at a time, to raise money for the National Health Service. His small, purposeful steps inspired us all to have **grit** during that very difficult time when so many people died from the virus. Captain Tom had survived many losses in his life but with his mindset he very clearly became the **boss of loss**. He always optimistically said, 'tomorrow will be a good day.' And in his book about his life and loss he said, 'and if tomorrow is my last day, if all those I loved are waiting for me, then that tomorrow will be a good day too.' Captain Tom died of coronavirus and pneumonia on the day I was finishing writing this book. It felt very sad that such a trusted friend to the world, everyone's grandad, was now gone. The relationship cannot be broken by death – he will be with us always. He recorded a version of a song called *You'll Never Walk Alone*. It got to number one – the oldest person ever to have a number-one record. The words to that song are so important.

You are not alone

You have had to face a very big challenge early on in your life. I so wish this hadn't happened to you. However, you now belong to a group of people who had to face a **significant** loss as they were growing up. I suspect you may meet others your age who have also experienced grief. Look out for them, as there will be many young people who have experienced the death of a family member or friend in their childhood. You are not alone.

45,000 children are bereaved of a parent or sibling annually in the UK. That is 112 newly bereaved children each day. These numbers are for the death of a parent; the number would be much higher if we include deaths of grandparents, siblings, other family and friends.*

5.2 million children in the USA will experience the death of a parent or sibling before they reach the age of 18. By the age of 25 this number rises to 13.2 million.**

* winstonswish.org/?s=Facts+and+figures

** judishouse.org

There is no right or wrong way to grieve, you need to find your way. We are very nearly at the end of the book ... what was the most important part for you? Is there one thing you can take away and remind yourself on the tough days? Was there something that maybe made you smile? I hope you can keep adding to your **memory box** and digital stash of photos and films.

Grief will still be with you as you grow up. It will probably be with you forever. It becomes a part of you. As you get older, you will one day leave school, leave home and at some point, there's college or work to look forward to. From time-to-time, grief may tap you on the shoulder just like it did for Gemma when she won her silver medal at the London Olympics. But the truth is that people we love continue to live on inside of us. **Love never dies**, which is why I have dedicated this book to my gorgeous grandad who died oodles of years ago. His sudden death was my first – and it rocked my world.

Thank you for reading this book. I know it is not quite the same as other books. I hope it helps you and those adults who care about you. Keep it safe in your memory box with all your other treasures. Dip into it again when you need to and lend it to others if you think they may need to read it.

I also have a hunch that as you grow up you will want to help others who are perhaps earlier on in their grief journey. They will quickly know that you are **someone who truly understands** what they are going through. You will be able to listen to their situation and maybe suggest a few tips to reassure them that, no matter what . . .

THEY WILL BE OKAY,

just like you.

Remember
strength does **not** come from what you **can** do.

Real strength
comes from
overcoming
the things you thought
you could **not** do.

FURTHER SUPPORT

Listed below are some helplines and websites based in the UK that are very experienced at talking to parents concerned about a child or young person. I suggest that you ask an adult to call the helplines and look into what additional help may be available. You may also want to explore the 'Young People' sections of these websites – they include some great short films of young people talking about their experiences. There are also some moderated conversations for you to ask questions online. Some specialist services are also available to help children meet others who have been bereaved by specific circumstances such as suicide, military deaths or murder and manslaughter. I very much hope that you will have the opportunity to find any additional support you need either online or close to home.

Winston's Wish: Giving Hope to Grieving Children
08088 020 021 – www.winstonswish.org; help2makesense.org

Child Bereavement UK
0800 02 888 40 – www.childbereavementuk.org

CRUSE Bereavement Care
0808 808 1677 – www.hopeagain.org.uk

Grief Encounter
0808 802 0111 – www.griefencounter.org.uk

Child bereavement networks

In the UK and Ireland, there are two major networks for professional people who want to help bereaved children and young people. Both of their websites (listed below) have search functions to help you find support that is local to you.

www.childhoodbereavementnetwork.org.uk
www.childhoodbereavement.ie

Support outside the UK

Europe – http://bereavement.eu

New Zealand – www.skylight.org.nz

India – https://palliumindia.org/2020/10/sukh-dukh-helpline

South Africa – www.khululeka.org

Australia – www.childhoodgrief.org.au

United States – www.dougy.org/

KEY SOURCES

Stokes J. Resilience and bereaved children: Helping a child to develop a resilient mind-set following the death of a parent. Bereavement Care 28 (1), 9-17, 2009.

Stroebe M.S. and Schut H. The Dual Process Model of Coping with Bereavement: rationale and description. Death Studies (1999). 23:197-224.

Tonkin L. Growing Around Grief: Another way of looking at recovery. Bereavement Care (1996); 15 (1):10

QUOTES (IN ORDER OF APPEARANCE)

Sir Bobby Charlton. Interview in *History of Football*, 10 December 2015. https://www.youtube.com/watch?v=4WRL3KDQsMU, accessed 17 May 2021.

Dawn French. *Dear Fatty* by Dawn French. (Arrow: 2009).

Nelson Mandela. 'Nelson Mandela, the father'. *The New Yorker*, 3 May 2013. https://www.newyorker.com/news/news-desk/nelson-mandela-the-father, accessed 17 May 2021.

Ruth Bader Ginsberg. *RBG*. (CNN Films 2018).

Joe Biden. *Promise Me, Dad: A Year of Hope, Hardship and Purpose* by Joe Biden. (Pan: 2017)

Jennifer Hudson. 'Moan', from the album JHUD (September 2014, RCA Records).

Louis Tomlinson. 'Louis Tomlinson on why he's done being sad, what inspired his second album, and his new London gig'. *The Telegraph*, 24 November 2020. https://www.telegraph.co.uk/music/artists/louis-tomlinson-done-sad-inspired-second-album-new-london-gig/, accessed 25 May 2021.

Tom Daley. 'How meditation made me a better diver.' Olympics.com, 19 May 2019. https://olympics.com/en/news/tom-daley-meditation-key-to-dream-olympic-gold-at-tokyo-2020, accessed 25 May 2021.

Gemma Gibson & Beryl Gibson. 'London 2012 Olympics: Judo silver medallist Gemma Gibbons - Live on the BBC? I can't, my hair's a mess.' *Evening Standard*, 3 August 2012. https://www.standard.co.uk/sport/sport-olympics/london-2012-olympics-judo-silver-medallist-gemma-gibbons-live-on-the-bbc-i-can-t-my-hair-s-a-mess-8004970.html, accessed 25 May 2021.

NOTE TO PARENTS/ADULTS

Although I have specifically written this book for a younger audience, I also hope that it may help you – the adults in their lives who care about them. Not only are you probably coping with your own grief right now, but you are also trying to stabilise family life. The warmth and boundaries you can provide for a child after such a big life event is invaluable. But please be easy on yourself, you may not always get things right as there really is no 'right' path. Hopefully this book will help you to find a path where you can all respect the different ways you all grieve and retain some sense of family togetherness.

RESOURCES

Listed below are some additional resources that you may find of interest. These short, informative books provide useful insights for adults supporting children. They are all available from Winston's Wish at https://www.winstonswish.org>publications

A Child's Grief Advice for adults supporting a child when someone has died

Never Too Young to Grieve Specific guidance for supporting children under five after the death of a parent or carer

You Just Don't Understand Guidance on supporting the individual needs of bereaved teenagers

We All Grieve Supporting children who have special educational needs and disabilities

Beyond the Rough Rock Practical advice for families in the immediate days and weeks when suicide has been the cause of death

Hope Beyond the Headlines Help and advice on supporting a child bereaved through murder or manslaughter

The Family Has Been Informed Supporting grieving children and young people from military families

As Big as it Gets Ideas on how to support a child when someone is seriously ill

WAY — Widowed & Young

This is the only national charity in the UK for men and women aged 50 or under when their partner died. The charity provides peer-to-peer support to young, widowed people - married or not, with or without children, whatever their sexual orientation - to adjust to life after the death of a partner. www.widowedandyoung.org.uk They have several books that their members have found helpful: https://www.widowedandyoung.org.uk/bereavement-support/useful-links/books-on-bereavement/

The Compassionate Friends Members have experienced the death of a child or children of many different ages and causes. Often, people who have suffered the loss of a child feel a bond with others in the same situation and wish to extend the hand of friendship. https://www.tcf.org.uk/content/helpline/

ACKNOWLEDGEMENTS

Dear Mum,

If I am going to thank anyone for being able to write a book on this topic – of course it must be you. It has been four years now since you died and frequently as I was writing, I found myself thinking – I wonder if *You Will Be Okay* might have helped you when your sister died and four years later when your mum died when you were 12? Would it perhaps have also helped your father to read it? All my life I was aware of the shadow of loss on your life – I know it left a big gap. I was always interested to meet other ABCs (Adults Bereaved as Children) and try to notice what had helped them to be strong and hopeful. Many of them were so incredibly insightful when writing this book.

ABC extraordinaire was my good friend David Scotland. David and another great pal, Peter Thompson, really held my hand on this writing project right from the get-go. Even when the words and grammar were very rough and certainly not ready, they held the vision and helped me to believe I could do it. I will never be able to thank them, and my other learned loyal friends, enough – Ali, Anthony, Becca, Carol, Di, Helena, Jo, John, Jackie, Janet, Kate, Katherine, Kath, Marilyn, Sam, Sue and Zoe – for reading it when it was truly messy: always finding something good to say while adding such important personal and professional perspectives.

The wonderful editors at Hachette – Laura and Sadie had me at 'hello' – as their straight-talking and supportive approach was completely aligned to what children and parents have taught me over the years. Talented designers Kat and Laura brought this book to life with their very special 'design magic'. I remember once you told me of an Irish saying, 'you meet people by chance at exactly the right time' – this was certainly true of Laurène, the brilliant French illustrator (who we later found out was two years old when her father died suddenly). Give sorrow words and pictures and it somehow feels much more manageable. It was a joy to see how the whole team at Hachette cared so much about the experience for the child reading their books.

Of course, the final acknowledgments are for the ones we love, no matter what. Your three wonderful grandchildren – Katie so naturally creative, encouraging and socially smart. Her thoughtful twin brother Matt – his genuine love of books made him an unexpected and rather brilliant thinking partner. Thank you, Matt, for saving me from myself in a few cringy moments in the book. And Conor my eldest – your first grandson, loving, smiley and always close by. Gifted with numbers rather than words – just like his dad. Yes, Ronan – I think he surprised you at how completely generous he has always been to me and my 'projects'. A good, fun, wise and super kind man. His loving mother Mary's own mother died shortly after Mary was born, and in the early days of Winston's Wish, Mary made a handwritten register of every child we saw, so that no child would ever be forgotten.

And finally, my dad. I am so pleased the piano aquarium made the cut – he would have loved that. Famous for his stories, projects and long nicknames ('Julie Anne, bread and jam, marmalade and treacle!') Hoping you and dad are now reunited and that a part of you feels a little reassured that children of this generation may find their way through the storms of grief a little more easily than was possible when you were young.

With love, **Julie Anne x**